TABLE OF CONTENTS

D1410068

Ask your friends to join you in 'Hands On' fun as you craft around the world. You'll love how exciting it can be to learn about different countries through their crafting traditions.

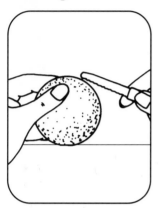

1. To cut the Styrofoam easily, rub the edge of a plastic knife with an old wax candle. Use the knife to cut through the foam with a sawing motion. Use a scrap piece of the Styrofoam to 'sand' any rough edges.

2. IMPORTANT! When you see the 'helping hand' symbol on a project page, it means you may need adult supervision to do the project. Always use care when using tools or a heat source. Be careful and safe!

3. Trace the patterns as needed onto the tracing paper. Lay the traced pattern on top of project surface. Place transfer, or graphite paper under the pattern then trace over design with a soft pencil, or crayon.

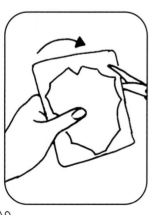

4. When cutting with a pair of scissors always work slowly and evenly. Hold the material you are cutting with the opposite hand, turning it toward the scissors as you cut.

5. When painting or working with messy materials, don't forget to protect your work surface with plastic or newspaper and your clothes with an apron or old shirt. Keep a roll of paper towels handy to wipe up spills.

Waxed Paper

6. To make sure paint doesn't seep through the shirts or fabric, use a piece of cardboard or wax paper inside the shirt or under fabric while painting. Tape the sleeves and excess shirt together at the back of the board.

7. Products used in each project are listed, but you can substitute with the supplies you might already have on hand. There are also some basic supplies that are used throughout the book: Paper clips, paper, toothpicks, etc.

8. For best results, always read and follow directions given on each product label. Some products may seem to do the same thing, but there may be important differences you need to know.

Get Ready for Your 'Hands On'
CRAFT ADVENTURE

Hey Kids!

Let's travel around the world with 'Hands On Crafts for Kids'. You'll learn about different cultures and countries through their crafts. But first you need to get ready...so, pack your bags and let's start with some travel crafts to make your journey special. We promise you'll have lots and lots of 'Hands-On' Fun!

Adventure Album Cover
by Patty Cox

Make a 3-D Album Cover using glue and paper in a very unique way. It will be the perfect place to store all the photographs you'll take on your trip!

Boat Pattern

RED

BLACK

BLACK

Place White tissue paper waves on the cover at the front of the boat.

Bemiss-Jason Corobuff®, Shredded Craft Confetti, Construction & Tissue Paper; Fiskars® Punches, Student Scissors & Paper Edgers; Darice® Embellishments & Raffia; Elmer's® Craft Bond™ Glue Stick, Gloss Decoupage Finish & Fun Dimensions™ Ice-A-Delic Cool Gel

You will need:

Two 9" x 12" Pieces of Royal Blue
  Metallic Corrugated Board
Construction Paper - Yellow, Red,
  Black, Orange and White
8" x 10" White Construction Paper
Hole and Star Punches
Tissue Paper - Red, Orange, Yellow,
  Pink, Light Blue, Dark Blue and White
White Confetti Paper Shreds
Icy Gel
Glue
Decoupage Finish
Decorative Edge Scissors
Red Raffia
Paintbrush
Wax Paper
Pencil
Scissors

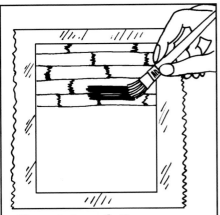

Glue strips of tissue paper to white paper to make the background for the ship.

Glue a 'V' of crumpled White tissue at front of boat.

1. Trace the entire pattern onto white construction paper. Cut around the outside edge of ship. Trace and cut red and black pattern pieces for hull and smokestack. Punch holes and stars in hull as shown, then glue onto main ship pattern.

2. Place ship on 8" x 10" white background paper (cover) then draw a line to mark the horizon. Set the ship aside.

3. Place cover on wax paper. Tear red, pink, orange, yellow and blue tissue paper into 1" wide strips. Brush decoupage finish onto the paper above horizon. Lay overlapping strips of red, pink, yellow and orange tissue paper onto wet surface to make different shades for the sunset. Glue blue tissue paper strips below the horizon for the water.

4. Brush decoupage finish over the back of the ship. Place on the cover. Tuck, then glue white confetti shreds under the top of the smoke stack. Brush decoupage finish over the whole page.

5. To make waves, crumple pieces of white tissue paper then glue on top of the blue. Make a "V" shape with one piece of crumpled paper and place at the front of the ship. Apply icy gel to the edge of the waves to make them sparkle. Set aside to dry. Trim edge of paper with decorative edge scissors then glue onto blue corrugated paper (coruboard).

6. Punch 3 holes into the same channel on the long edge of the coruboard about $\frac{1}{2}$" from the edge. Punch one hole about 2" from the top, one hole 2" from the bottom and the third hole in the center. Place on top of second piece of coruboard, wrong sides together. Mark holes then punch holes in second piece. Tie boards together with raffia.

7. Write, stamp or stencil the title onto a $1\frac{1}{2}$" x $3\frac{1}{2}$" piece of yellow paper. Glue onto orange paper then trim with decorative scissors. Glue to the front. Decorate with buttons if desired.

Bulletin Board
by Kim Thomas

A bulletin board is a great place to post souvenirs from your trip. Decorate the edge with a flag from each country, you can even add some extra ones to make it even more colorful!

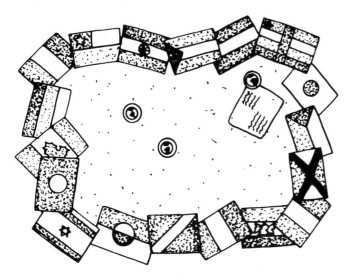

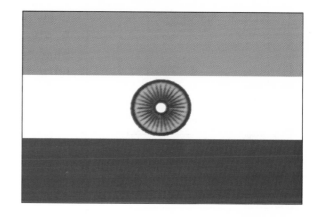

You will need:
12" x 18" x 1" Piece of Styrofoam
Foam Sheets - White, Red, Yellow,
  Royal Blue, Black and Green
Six ⅝" Wood Button Bowls
Six 10mm Flat Pad Earring Posts
Six World Stickers
Light Blue Non-Aerosol Spray Color,
  or Paint
Fine Tip Permanent Markers
Tacky Glue
Scissors
Pencil
2" x 3" Piece of Card

1. Color the front of styrofoam sheet Light Blue with either non-aerosol spray paint or acrylic paint.

2. Choose a background color of foam for a flag. Using card as a template, cut a 2" x 3" rectangle from the foam sheet.

3. Trace flag patterns onto paper. Working with one flag at a time, cut pattern apart then place each piece on corresponding color of foam. Cut out foam pieces then glue them onto the flag.

4. Emblems can be drawn on flags with a permanent marker. Glue flags around the edge of bulletin board.

5. Glue earring posts to the inside of wooden bowls. Let dry then place a sticker on top of each one to make a thumb tack.

Note: Use these flag designs and those found at the beginning of each section. You'll also find some other flags on the cover of the book. Check your library to see if you can find the names of the countries that they represent.

India

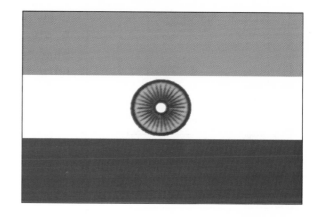

Morocco

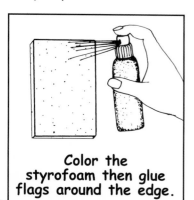

Color the styrofoam then glue flags around the edge.

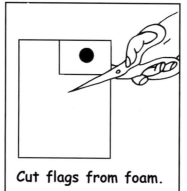

Cut flags from foam.

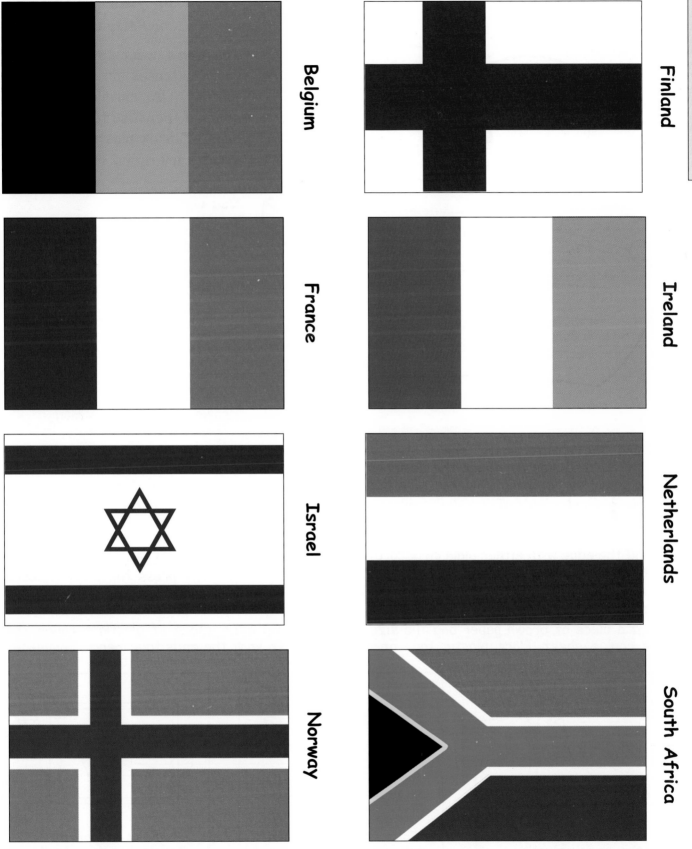

Finland

Belgium

Ireland

France

Netherlands

Israel

South Africa

Norway

Darice® Foamies, Earring Posts, Wood Bowls; Delta Ceramcoat® Acrylic Paint & Color Mist;
Dow Styrofoam® Brand Plastic Foam; Elmer's® Craft Bond™ Tacky Glue; Fiskars® Scissors;
Dixon Redisharp® Fine Point Markers

Tag your Bags

by Patty Cox

You won't want to lose any of your suitcases on such a long journey. Use shrink plastic and colored pencils to "tag your bags". Shrink plastic works like magic - try it and see!

You will need:
Frosted Shrink Plastic
Colored Pencils
Plastic Lacing
Black Fine Permanent
  Tip Marker
Scissors
Hole Punch
Cookie Sheet
Toaster Oven
Brown Paper Grocery Bag

1. Place the shrink plastic sheet over your design, frosted side up. Trace the design with black pencil or permanent marker. Use design shown, flags, or create your own design!

2. Color design with colored pencils on the frosted side of the plastic sheet then cut around the edge with either plain or decorative edge scissors.

3. Use a punch to make a hole in a corner of each tag.

4. Cut a piece of brown paper bag the size of your cookie sheet. Place plastic tags on the paper covered cookie sheet, colored side up. Heat in a toaster oven or conventional oven pre-heated to 300 degrees for 1-3 minutes.

5. When pieces lay flat, allow an additional 30 seconds of baking time to complete the process.

6. Carefully remove the brown paper from the cookie sheet. Lightly press the plastic pieces flat with a pad of paper for about 15 seconds until the plastic has cooled.

7. Thread a 12" piece of plastic through the hole then knot the ends together to complete.

Trace design onto
the shrink plastic.

Color the design then
cut out and make hole.

Bake on paper
covered cookie sheet

Darice® Plastic Lacing; Dixon Redimark® Fine Tip Markers;
Fiskars® Scissors & Punches; Prang® Colored Pencils; K&B Innovations Shrinky Dinks®

Add-On Travel Bag

by Laurie Lazzaro Knowlton

Each country or state has its own special shape. Add the shape of each country or state that you have visited to make your own unique travel bag.

You will need:
Canvas Tote Bag
Fabric Scraps
Scissors
Fabric Glue
Colored Dimensional Glue
Pencil
Brush
Puzzle Pieces for Patterns

1. Trace the outline of a country from a map onto tracing paper, or use a single country puzzle piece as a pattern. Place patterns on fabric. Trace around the outline with pencil then cut out.

2. Brush fabric glue onto the back of the fabric then place it on your canvas bag. Press down, making sure to press out any bubbles.

3. Outline the edges of the shape with colored glue. Let dry.

4. Add the shape of a country or state that you visited after each vacation. You can also add shapes of states and countries that you either flew over, or drove through.

Hint: Another idea would be to add the shapes of states and countries where friends and family live.

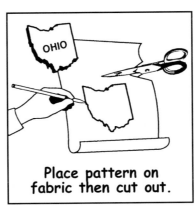

Place pattern on fabric then cut out.

Smooth fabric piece in place on bag.

Outline shape with dimensional glue.

Add more shapes as desired.

Elmer's® Acid-Free Craft Bond™ Fabric & Paper Glue & Squeeze Creations™;
Fiskars® Scissors; Dixon Ticonderoga® Pencils

Sea Mist-Shirt
by Tracia Ledford-Williams

What could be more fitting to wear on your ocean voyage than a sprayed shirt! This one has been sprayed with paint and not the ocean. Add some sea creatures and you'll have something fun to wear for all occasions.

You will need:
Non-Aerosol Spray Paint -
  Blue, Yellow and Pink
Clear Contact® Paper
Silver Glitter Fabric Paint
T-Shirt or Sweat Shirt
Scissors
Black Fine Tip Permanent Pen
Shirt Board or Cardboard
Flat Paintbrush

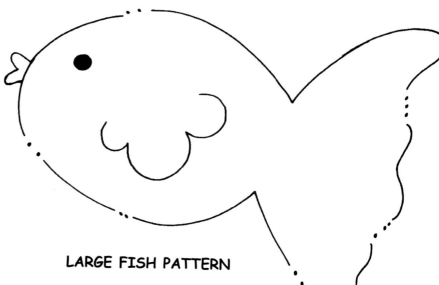

LARGE FISH PATTERN

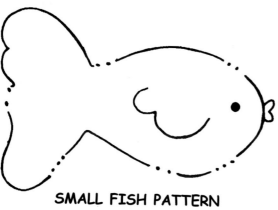

SMALL FISH PATTERN

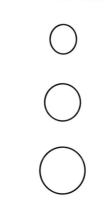

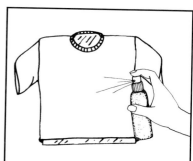

Mist shirt with non-aerosol spray paint.

1. Place a shirt board, or cardboard inside the shirt.

2. Cover work area with newspaper or plastic to protect surface from overspray.

3. Randomly mist shirt with yellow then pink. Allow paint to dry.

4. Trace fish shapes onto contact paper then cut out. Peel away the backing paper then stick the fish shapes onto the painted shirt. Mist the fish and the entire shirt lightly with blue. Remove the fish shapes and allow to dry.

5. Use the black marker to outline the fish and to draw bubbles coming from the fish. Draw a mouth, eye and gill on each fish.

6. Paint the waves and bubbles with silver glitter fabric paint.

7. Allow the paint to cure for 6 days, then launder inside out. Color does not need to be heat set. Once the paint has dried it is there forever!

Use a flat brush to paint waves and bubbles.

**Delta Color Mist™, Starlite Glitter™;
Dixon Redimark® Fine Tip Markers; Fiskars® Scissors**

Join Our Craft Adventure to
CHINA

Discover the beauty of China and make your own

- Tangram Set • Dragon Dance Stick • Chinese Dragon Mask • Hanging Lantern • Panda Picture • Magpie Wind Chime

Tangram Fun
Courtesy of FamilyFun

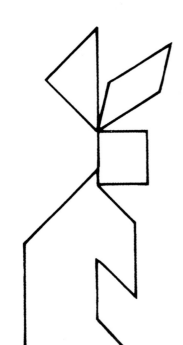

In China, Tangram is called *chi chao ban*, or the seven boards of cunning. The game is said to have originated over 4,000 years ago! Build your own tangram and you will soon discover why it has lasted so long.

You will need:
Square Sheets of Paper
Scissors
Glue
Cardstock

1. To make a seven-piece tangram, start with a square piece of white or colored paper, any size. Fold it diagonally to make a triangle. Unfold then cut along the fold line.

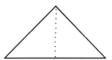

2. Fold one of the triangles in half then cut it apart along the fold line to make two small triangles.

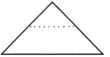

3. Fold the large triangle so that the top point touches the center of the long side. Cut on the fold to make a small triangle and a quadrangle.

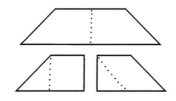

4. Fold the quadrangle in half then cut along fold line. Fold point of one of these pieces as shown then cut along fold line to form a small triangle and a square. Fold the remaining pieces as shown then cut on fold line.

5. To make more rigid, glue the seven pieces of paper onto the cardstock then cut out.

Rules of the Game:
Use the tangram pieces to play a game with your friends. Pick out one of the tangram pictures and study it carefully. The first person to duplicate the design is the winner. Play by yourself by using a timer to see how long it takes to duplicate the designs, or challenge your family with tangram puzzles. Arrange the pieces into a tangram figure on a piece of paper. Draw around the outline, remove the pieces then color the design. See how long it takes other players to recreate your figure using their tangram pieces.

Bemiss-Jason Origami Paper;
Fiskars® Paper Edgers; Elmer's® Paper Glue

Dragon Dance Stick
by Kim Thomas

Join the New Year celebrations and chase the "sun" with your own dance stick. If the sun was ever caught, the Chinese believed it would go out! The dance is to celebrate the sun and spring rain.

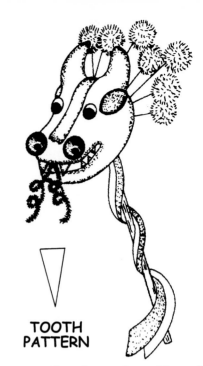

You will need:

$4\frac{1}{2}$" Styrofoam Egg	White Foam Sheet
Two 1" Styrofoam Balls	Tissue Paper - Yellow,
$1\frac{1}{2}$" Styrofoam Ball	Orange, Lt. Orange & Red
Tinsel Stems - Gold, Green	Tacky Glue
and 3 Blue	Paper Glue Gel
Seven 1" Tinsel Pom Poms	18" of $\frac{1}{4}$" Dowel
in assorted colors	Decorative Scissors
Two 20mm Wiggle Eyes	Black Paint
	Paintbrush

TOOTH PATTERN

1. Press the pointed end of the styrofoam egg against a hard surface to flatten. Cut a 1" x $\frac{1}{2}$" piece from the flattened end. Cut this piece in half for ears.

2. Cut the $1\frac{1}{2}$" styrofoam ball in half then squeeze each piece into a football shape for cheek bones. Flatten opposite sides of two 1" styrofoam balls for nostrils.

3. Glue the dowel into base of egg. Flatten area for forehead with fingertips. Glue ears and nostrils in place. Use toothpicks if necessary to hold pieces in place until the glue dries. Make the holes for each nostril with a paintbrush handle.

4. Cut tissue paper into 6" x 8" squares then tear into small pieces. Brush glue gel onto the styrofoam. Using orange for ears and nostrils, red for mouth and yellow and lt. orange for the head, completely cover the styrofoam with pieces of tissue paper. Brush surface liberally with the glue gel.

5. Cut a 1" x 6" strip of red tissue with decorative scissors then glue down the center of head.

6. Twist the ends of two blue glitter stems together, then wrap around dowel to curl. Glue the twisted end into the mouth. Cut remaining glitter stems in half. Set one piece aside then glue a pom pom to the end of each of the seven stems. Glue stems into the back of dragon's head for a mane.

7. Cut eight teeth and two fangs from white foam and glue to mouth. Paint inside of nostrils black. Glue eyes in place.

8. Using decorative scissors, cut the remaining tissue into $2\frac{1}{2}$" x 30" streamers. Group ends together and secure with remaining piece of glitter stem. Glue end of stems into styrofoam below mane.

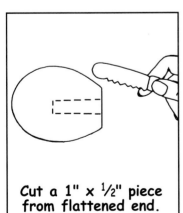

Cut a 1" x $\frac{1}{2}$" piece from flattened end.

Glue ears and nostrils in place on head.

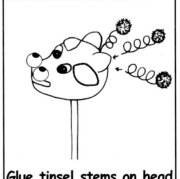

Glue tinsel stems on head and fangs to mouth.

FANG PATTERN

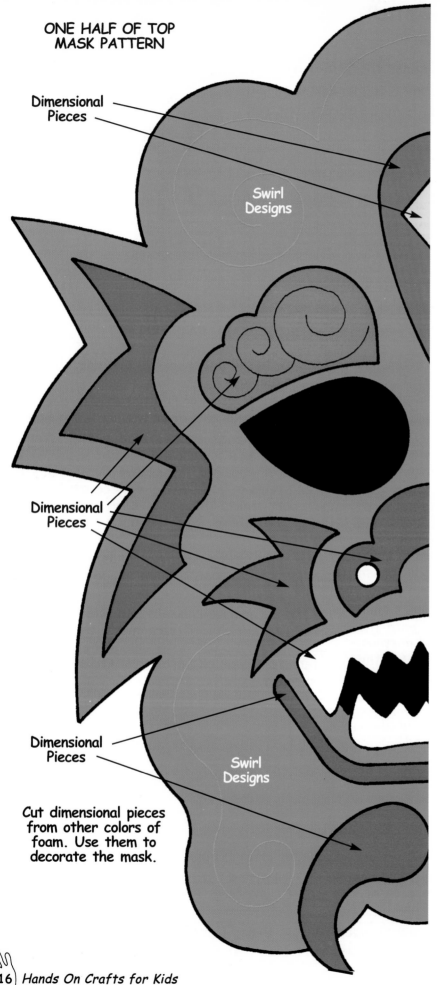

Dimensional
Pieces

Swirl
Designs

Dimensional
Pieces

Dimensional
Pieces

Swirl
Designs

Cut dimensional pieces
from other colors of
foam. Use them to
decorate the mask.

Chinese Dragon Mask
by Patty Cox

When the first New Moon enters the sign of Aquarius it's time to celebrate the Chinese New Year. Farmers and merchants perform lion and dragon dances to bring prosperity for the future.

1. Trace pattern for mask base onto a folded piece of paper with center of pattern on fold. Cut out including areas for eyes and mouth and slits for nose. Unfold paper to give full pattern. Place on foam then trace around cutting lines with a marker. Cut out mask base. Use pointed scissors to cut out holes for eyes and mouth and a slit for the nose.

2. Punch a hole in each side. Overlap and staple "V" cutouts on sides, top and bottom of mask.

3. Make a pattern for the top of the mask in the same way. Place on foam then cut out. Use the base pattern to make slits for nose, eyes and mouth openings.

4. Transfer the designs for the dimensional pieces onto paper. Lay patterns onto colored pieces of foam and trace over design with a ball point pen. The impression will remain on the foam. Cut out. Glue some of the dimensional pieces to a contrasting color of foam. Cut around the second color with the decorative edge scissors about ½" away from edge. Glue shapes to front of mask with the glue stick.

5. Trace pattern for swirl designs on front of mask then paint with glitter glue and markers.

6. Decorate with dots of glitter glue, sequins, rhinestones, mirrors or punched foam shapes.

7. Glue mask top to base matching holes for eyes and mouth. Tie the elastic through holes in sides.

You will need:
Foam - Red, Blue, Fuchsia, Aqua, White & Orange
18" of 2mm Elastic Cord
Decorative Scissors
Glitter Glue
Glue Stick
Tacky Glue
Embellishments - Sequins, Rhinestones, etc.
Fine Tip Markers
Stapler

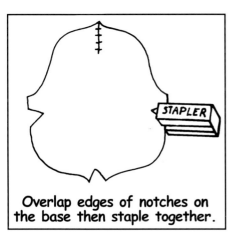

Overlap edges of notches on the base then staple together.

Cut out areas for eyes on top and bottom pieces.

Darice® Foamies & Embellishments; Dixon Redimark® Fine Tip Markers; Elmer's® Fun Dimensions™ Glitter Gel, Craft Bond™ Glue Stick & Tacky Glue; Fiskars® Paper Edgers & Punches

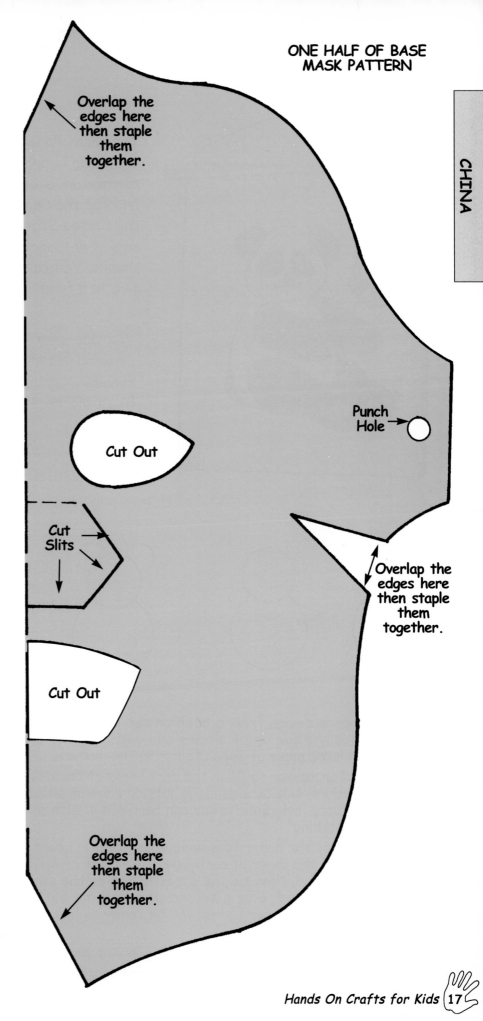

ONE HALF OF BASE MASK PATTERN

CHINA

Overlap the edges here then staple them together.

Punch Hole

Cut Out

Cut Slits

Overlap the edges here then staple them together.

Cut Out

Overlap the edges here then staple them together.

Panda
by Cecille Diez

The Giant Panda lives in the mountainous areas of China and is protected by Chinese law because it is so rare. It is one of China's most beloved animals. In 1972 the Chinese government gave two pandas to the United States as a gesture of goodwill. See how easy it is to make a drawing of a Panda using simple shapes. You can make one for yourself and one to give to a friend.

You will need:
Drawing Paper
Pencils
Black Markers
Dowels
String
Glue

Make dash lines for fur.

To fill in larger areas, use cross-hatch lines.

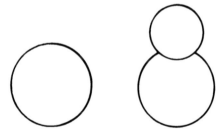   

1. Select a panda design from a book or see illustration. The basic design is actually made up of circles and ovals. Lightly sketch the design onto a large piece of paper following the pattern.

2. Use a pencil or marker to fill in the dark areas of the design. Make small lines (dashes) side by side along outside edge of shapes to give your panda a furry look. Solid areas can be filled in with a technique called "crosshatching".

3. Glue the top of the paper to a wood dowel that is about 1" longer than the width of the paper at each side. Tie a piece of string around one end of the dowel, then tie the opposite end of the string to the other end of the dowel. Glue a second dowel to the bottom of the paper for stability and your banner will be ready to hang.

DOWEL
Glue top of paper to a wooden dowel.

Bemiss-Jason Art Kraft® Paper;
Dixon Redimark® Permanent Markers & Ticonderoga Pencils.

Magpie Wind Chime
by Kim Thomas

The Magpie is a traditional Chinese symbol of joy. Be sure to read the ancient Chinese fairy tale *"The Princess and the Cowherd"* when making this project. It is about the Magpies who spread their wings to make a bridge to join two friends.

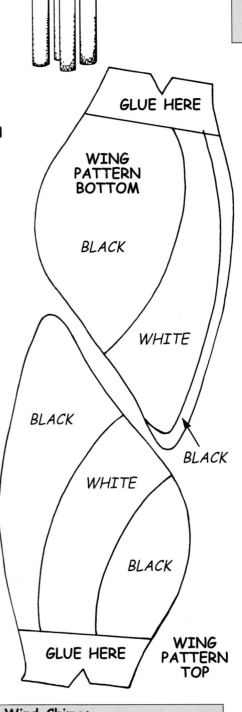

You will need:
3" Styrofoam Egg
1½" Styrofoam Ball
9" x 12" Magicraft Paper
Acrylic Paint - Black, Red, Bright Green, Medium Blue
Four 2" Pear Head Pins
Eye Pin
6mm Aluminum Wind Chimes Waxed Linen
Thread
Gesso
Tacky Glue
Flat Paint Brush

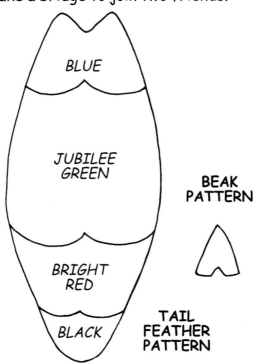

BLUE

JUBILEE GREEN

BRIGHT RED

BLACK

BEAK PATTERN

TAIL FEATHER PATTERN

GLUE HERE

WING PATTERN BOTTOM

BLACK

WHITE

BLACK

BLACK

WHITE

BLACK

GLUE HERE

WING PATTERN TOP

1. Trace patterns for tail, beak and wings onto cardboard then cut out.

2. Glue a toothpick into the 1½" ball then glue the ball into the small end of the egg to make body. Insert then glue notched end of tail into the ball at a slight angle. Glue the wings to each side of body and beak to head. To make a hanger, glue the eye pin into the center of the bird's back. Thread a 6" piece of waxed linen through the hanger then knot the ends together.

3. Cut magicraft paper lengthwise into ½" wide strips. Lightly moisten one side of strip with wet paintbrush. With moist side down, press the strips around the bird overlapping when necessary. When entire bird is covered, set aside to dry.

4. Cover bird with two coats of gesso, letting it dry between coats. Paint the bird as shown on the patterns.

5. Draw a ¾" square on the bottom of the bird then push one eye pin into each corner. Tie remaining waxed linen through one eye pin leaving a 3" tail. Thread one chime onto the waxed linen then thread the linen through the next eye pin letting chimes hang 2" below the bird. Continue stringing chimes in this manner until all four are strung. You will now be back at the first eye pin. Thread the waxed linen through the pin then knot both tails together to finish. Cut off excess then push pins into the bird as far as possible.

Bemiss-Jason Magicraft™; Darice® Pins and Wind Chime; Delta Ceramcoat® Acrylic Paint and Gesso; Dow Styrofoam® Brand Plastic Foam.

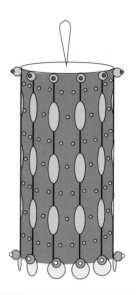

Hanging Lantern
by Patty Cox

During the full moon of the Chinese New Year, houses and lamp poles were decorated with paper lanterns. These can easily be simulated using two-tone paper, scissors and glue.

1¾" FOLDS

18"

12"

PIN   **BEAD**   SEQUIN

You will need:
12" x 18" Two-Tone Paper
Two 5" Styrofoam Disks
12" Plastic Lacing
18 Faceted 10mm Plastic Beads
9 Gold 20mm Sequins
Decorative Scissors
Hole Punch
18 Round Head Straight Pins
White Glue
Glue Stick
Toothpick
Craft Stick

1. Starting at narrow end, fold two-colored paper into accordion folds every 1¾".
2. Cut half circles out of folded edges and punch holes in paper as shown. If folded paper is too thick to work with, punch one folded layer at a time.
3. Open up folded paper then crease all folds in same direction.
4. Punch a hole in the center of one styrofoam disc with a toothpick twisting a little to enlarge the hole.
5. Fold plastic lacing in half and thread both ends through the hole. Knot ends together. Thread a toothpick through the knot to keep the knot from pulling through the hole. Tie a knot in the lacing on the other side of the disc.
6. With the light color to the inside, glue top edge of the paper around the edge of one disc. Glue the bottom edge of the paper around second disc. Glue edges of the paper together where they overlap.
7. Thread a bead and a sequin onto a straight pin. Insert the pin into the styrofoam base through the paper, using crease marks as a guide. Thread a bead onto a straight pin then insert it into the top of the lantern, through the paper in the same manner.

1¾"
FOLDS

Actual Size Cutting and Punching Patterns

FOLDED EDGE   FOLDED EDGE

Bemiss-Jason Fadeless® Duet Paper; Elmer's® Craft Bond Tacky Glue & Glue Stick; Darice® Plastic Lacing, Sequins & Beads; Dow Styrofoam® Brand Plastic Foam; Fiskars® Scissors & Punches

Join Our Craft Adventure to the
UNITED KINGDOM

Have a 'Jolly Good Time' making these fun crafts:

- Easy Tatting • Snip Shots
- Weaving Loom • Knitting Spools • Afternoon Tea

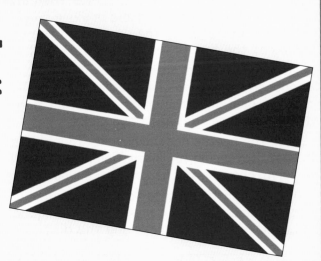

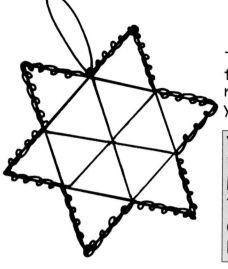

Easy Tatting
by Julie McGuffee

Tatting, crochet and hairpin lace are techniques for knotting thread to make "lace-like" doilies for the home and embellishments for clothing. Traditional tatting is a long process, but you'll find it fast and fun with this easy technique.

You will need:

White Cotton Cord or Yarn	Decorative Glue
Large Eye Plastic Needle	Wax Paper
7 Craft Picks	6" Styrofoam Disc
6 Pony Beads	Pencil
Fabric Stiffener	Paintbrush

SLIP KNOT

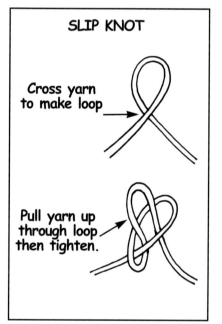

Cross yarn to make loop

Pull yarn up through loop then tighten.

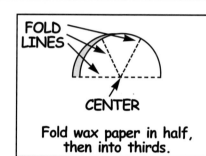

FOLD LINES

CENTER

Fold wax paper in half, then into thirds.

Place looped yarn on top of craft sticks and pony beads.

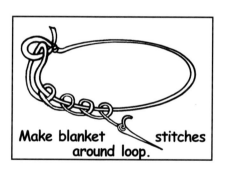

Make blanket stitches around loop.

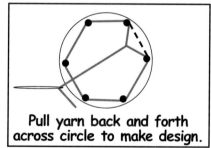

Pull yarn back and forth across circle to make design.

1. Trace around the styrofoam disc onto wax paper, then cut out the circle. Fold the circle in half. Fold in half again to mark the center then into thirds. Unfold the wax paper circle then place on top of the styrofoam disc. Hold in place by placing a craft pick in the center and at each fold line, approximately ½" from the edge. Push the craft sticks well into the styrofoam so that only 1" is showing at the top. Break off any tips that appear through the bottom of the disc.

2. Place a pony bead over each craft stick. Make a slip knot in one end of the yarn then thread the opposite end onto the needle. Pull needle and yarn through the slip knot to make a loop then place the loop over the craftsticks. Pull tightly so that the loop rests on top of the pony beads with the slip knot between two picks.

3. Using the needle and yarn make "blanket" style stitches around the loop, ending at the original slip knot. Referring to illustration pull the yarn backwards and forwards across the circle. Thread the yarn through stitches on outer ring to keep it in place. Tie the ends together to finish.

4. Dip the paintbrush into fabric stiffener and thoroughly saturate the yarn snowflake avoiding the craftpicks. Let dry completely then squeeze decorative glue over the top of the yarn. Let dry then remove from the picks and the disc.

Dow Styrofoam® Brand Plastic Foam; Elmer's® Craft Bond™ Fabric Stiffener & Fun Dimensions™ Ice-A-Delic™ Cool Gel; Fiskars® Creative Works® Paint Brushes

You will need:

Tea Cup and Saucer
Mug
Glass and Tile Paint -
  Red, White, Black,
  Green, Fuchsia,
  Yellow and Purple
Surface Conditioner
Clear Gloss Glaze
#12 Flat Paintbrush
#0 Liner Brush
Old Scruffy Brush
New Pencil with Eraser
Toothpicks
Compressed Sponge
Scissors

Afternoon Tea
by Tracia Ledford-Williams

A trip to England would not be complete without a cup of tea. Try these new paints on a cup and saucer or mug. The design is perfect for afternoon tea or an after-school snack.

Tea Cup and Saucer

1. Brush surface conditioner over area to be painted. Dip scruffy brush in Green then White. Pounce brush up and down to create foliage. Dip a pencil eraser into Fuchsia paint and make dots for flowers.

2. Using a toothpick add groups of three Yellow dots and single White and Purple dots. Allow paint to dry thoroughly then seal with a thin, even coat of gloss glaze.

Teacher Mug

1. Cut apple and ½" square designs from compressed sponge. Dip in water to expand. Squeeze out excess water.

2. Dip apple shape into Red paint and use to paint apples around the mug. Use square sponge to paint Green checks. Use paintbrush handle to paint a Yellow dot between the checks. Paint a Yellow highlight, Green leaf and a Black stem on the apple. Allow paint to dry thoroughly then seal with a thin, even coat of gloss glaze.

Note: Allow paint to cure for 10 days before using.

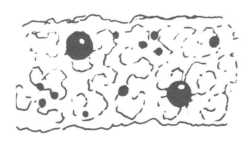

FOLIAGE AND FLOWERS PATTERN

APPLE PATTERN

Delta Air-Dry PermEnamel™ Glass & Tile Paint, Surface Conditioner & Glaze

Snip Shots
by Julie McGuffee

Do you ever wonder what it might be like to be a Beefeater or a Palace Guard for the Queen? Use these great cut outs and your photographs and leave the rest to your imagination!

You will need:

Markers or Crayons - Red, Orange, Yellow, Black, Brown
Fine Permanent Black Marker
4" x 9" Styrofoam
Dark Grey Acrylic Paint
Glue
Scissors

Paintbrush
Heavyweight Paper
Tracing Paper
Graphite Paper
Pencil
Plastic Knife
Color Copies of Photographs

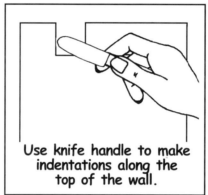

Use knife handle to make indentations along the top of the wall.

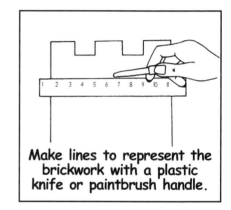

Make lines to represent the brickwork with a plastic knife or paintbrush handle.

1. Trace then transfer the Beefeater and Palace Guard pictures onto heavy paper. Trace over the lines with a black permanent marker then color with markers or crayons. Leave the area for the face blank. Cut out around the outside lines then cut the hat from the figures and set aside.

2. Cut your face from the color copy of your photograph then glue onto the face area of the guard. Glue the hat onto your head! Glue the finished figures to a folded piece of paper to make a notecard, or make a castle wall:

 a. Press the handle of the knife into the top edge of the styrofoam rectangle to make indentations ½" x ½" one inch apart along the top. Use the knife handle or a paintbrush handle to make the horizontal and vertical lines on the front of the styrofoam to represent the brickwork on the wall.

 b. Paint the styrofoam grey. Use lots of paint on your brush and pounce the brush up and down, if necessary to achieve good coverage. Let dry, then glue your figure to the front.

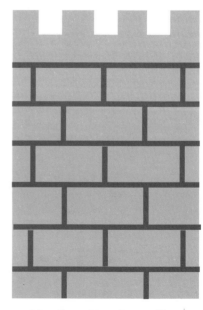

BRICKWORK PATTERN

Glue your
photo here

Glue your
photo here

Dow Styrofoam® Brand Plastic Foam; Dixon Redimark® Fine Tip Markers; Prang® Fun Pro™ Crayons & Washable Markers™; Fiskars® Student Scissors & Creative Works™ Paintbrush

Over and Under Weaving
by Julie McGuffee

There is nothing more British than woolens and fibers. Use the same age old techniques to weave your own fabric on a loom made from cardboard, styrofoam and craftsticks!

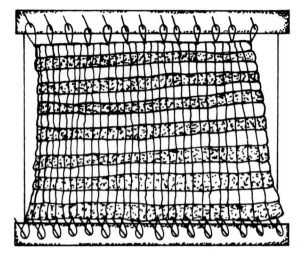

You will need:
8" x 11" Stiff Cardboard
Two 8" x 2" pieces of
  Styrofoam
15 Mini Craft Sticks
Tacky Glue
6" Plastic Yarn Needle
3" Plastic Needle
Assorted Colors of Yarn
12" Ruler
Scissors

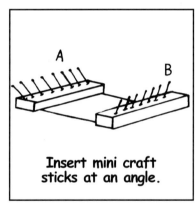

Insert mini craft sticks at an angle.

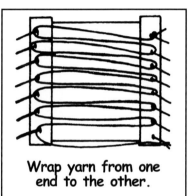

Wrap yarn from one end to the other.

Weave yarn up and down across loom.

1. Securely glue one strip of styrofoam to each end of the cardboard. Let dry overnight.

2. Push the craft sticks into the styrofoam at an angle. Place one inch apart starting 1" from the edge. Repeat on the opposite end, this time starting ½" from the end. You will have 8 craft sticks on side A and 7 craft sticks on side B.

3. Using approximately two yards of yarn, tie one end to the first craft stick on side A. Stretch the yarn across the board to the first craft stick on side B. Loop around and stretch the yarn back across the board and pass around the second stick on side A. Continue wrapping the yarn across then tie off yarn around the last stick.

4. Thread the yarn needle with approximately two yards of yarn then, starting 2" from the top begin weaving from one side to the other by pulling the yarn over the first strand of yarn, under the second, over the third, etcetera until you reach the other side. Turn the loom around and repeat. Use the yarn needle to push the strands of yarn together as you weave backwards and forwards. Change colors as often as you like by tying the end of one color to the beginning of the next color.

5. To finish, snip the yarn behind each craft stick then tie two strands together. Thread the ends of yarn on the sides onto the small needle one at a time and pull through the back of your project to secure, or tie knots using the end of one piece of yarn and the beginning of the next.

Bemiss-Jason Assorted Yarns & Yarn Needle;
Dow Styrofoam® Brand Plastic Foam; Fiskars® School Ruler & Student Scissors

Knitting Spool
by Julie McGuffee

Knit yards and yards of cord with what is commonly called a "Dolly Bobbin". Also known as French knitting, you can use the cording to make all kinds of things. You can even use the cord to decorate your clothing!

You will need:
Four 1" Nails (without a head)
Yarn of your choice (thick yarn
   is not advisable)

3" Large Eye Plastic Needle
One $\frac{1}{2}$" x $2\frac{1}{4}$" Spool
Fabric Glue
Hammer

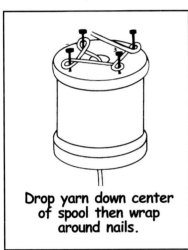

Drop yarn down center of spool then wrap around nails.

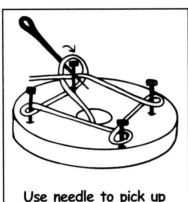

Use needle to pick up yarn over loop to make the stitch.

1. Carefully hammer four nails into the top of the spool as shown.

2. Decorate the spool by tightly wrapping with yarn. Glue ends to secure.

3. Thread the end of yarn through the needle, then drop the needle through the hole in the spool from the top. Remove the needle. While holding the end of the yarn at the bottom of the spool, loop the yarn around each nail, in a counter-clockwise direction.

4. Lay the yarn against the first nail, then use the needle to pick the looped yarn over the strand of yarn and over the top of the nail. Repeat until you have done this around all four nails. Stitches will be loose at this point. Continue making stitches around each nail. Pull the strand of yarn at the bottom of the spool each time you create two or three stitches. You'll be surprised how quickly your cord grows.

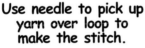

Coil one yard of cord to make a coaster.

5. When your cord is long enough, cut the yarn 12" from the top of the spool. Thread the end of the yarn onto the needle, then use the needle to lift each stitch off the nail. Pull the yarn through the stitches to secure. Pull tightly together to close loop. Pull the cord out of the bobbin from the bottom.

6. Coil approximately one yard of cord to make a coaster. Keeping coils tightly together, thread the piece of yarn at the end of the cord onto the needle then pull through the coils to the center to keep them in place. Squeeze a liberal amount of fabric glue between the coils. Let dry overnight.

Bemiss-Jason Assorted Yarn & Needle;
Darice® Wood Spool; Elmer's® Craft Bond™ Fabric Glue

Join Our Craft Adventure to
AUSTRALIA

G'Day Mate...
Remember to watch out for the 'crocks' while you are here in the Australian Outback!

- Cave Painting
- Boomerang
- Woolly Sheep
- Koalas
- Pony Bead Crocodile

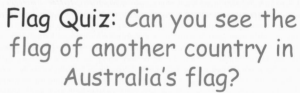

Flag Quiz: Can you see the flag of another country in Australia's flag?

Pony Bead Crocodile
Courtesy of Darice® Creative Crafts

Who can think about Australia without thinking about crocodiles! At least you won't have to wrestle with this one! Pony bead animals are fun to make - you could easily make enough to populate the whole outback.

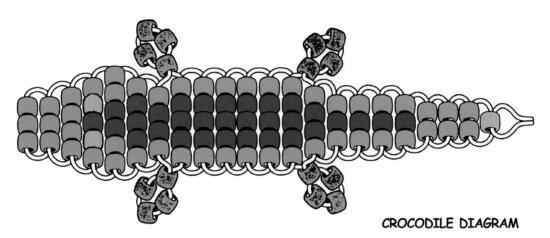

CROCODILE DIAGRAM

You will need:
Pony Beads -
  64 Green
  32 Olive
   3 Shiny Green
2½ yards Clear Plastic Lacing,
  or ¼" Ribbon

STEP 1

First Row: Fold cord in half then string 3 pony beads onto center of the cord.

Second Row: Thread 3 beads onto one side of lace then thread the other end of the lace through the same 3 beads in the opposite direction. (Step 1).

Third - Seventh Row: Using diagram as a guide, repeat threading beads in the same manner.

Feet: Thread 4 Olive beads onto lace then thread the lace back through the first Olive bead. (Step 2).

Eighth Row: Thread beads onto lace. Make opposite foot then thread lace through same beads. (Step 3).

Repeat this technique to the end referring to illustration for bead placement. Tie ends of lace together. Attach to a key chain ring, or zipper pull if desired.

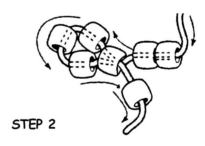

STEP 2

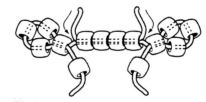

STEP 3

Darice® Pony Beads & Plastic Lacing

Boomerang

Cecille Diez

There are two kinds of boomerangs, the non-returning which were used for hunting and the returning boomerangs used mostly for sport. They are often decorated with designs important to the Aboriginal legends and traditions.

You will need:
Foam Board or Cardboard
Colored Markers
Craft Knife

Use the pattern below to make your boomerang. For other design ideas, look in your encyclopedia under "Aborigine, Art".

1. Sketch the boomerang shape onto foam board or cardboard then cut out.

2. Using a combination of different geometric designs and colors, create your own traditional style boomerang pattern. Aboriginal art also reflected elements of nature. You will find designs of leaves, twigs, birds' footprints and pawprints. You may want to include some of these in your boomerang patterns also.

3. Display your boomerang by hanging it from the ceiling or tall bookshelf. You can make an entire collection, each with a different design featuring lots of colors, or use only a few colors and the art of repetitive patterns to create interest.

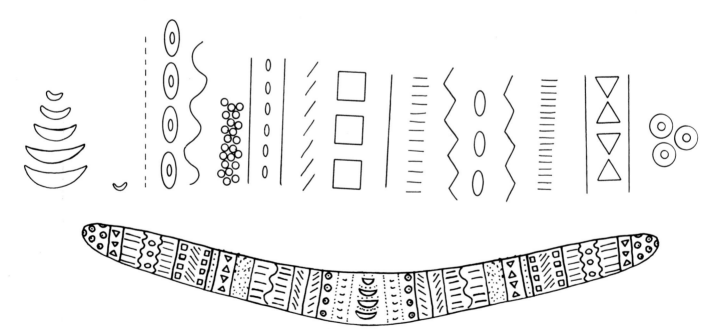

Dixon Redimark® Permanent Markers; Fiskars® Razor Knife

Cave Painting
by Tracia Ledford-Williams

Australia's native inhabitants, the Aborigines, left their mark through their paintings on rocks and the walls of caves. The designs feature repetitive geometric shapes and mythical beings. Use these ideas to paint your own rocks and leave your mark for the future.

You will need:
Acrylic Paint - Black,
  Butter Cream, Royal
  Fuchsia, Bahama
  Purple, Empire Gold
  and Golden Brown
Satin Exterior Varnish
Rocks
Tracing Paper
Graphite Paper
Pencil
Paintbrushes

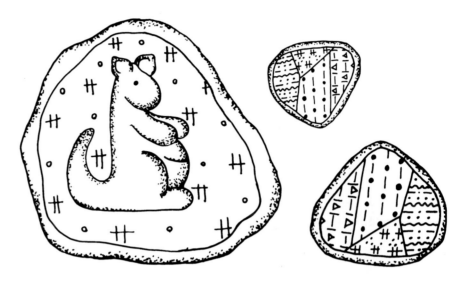

Use these patterns to paint your own rocks:

1. Basecoat the rocks with either Butter Cream or Black. Divide painted area into sections then paint a different pattern in each section. Use simple lines, X's, dots and other geometric designs.
2. Trace then transfer Kangaroo pattern onto a rock. Paint Kangaroo Golden Brown, outline with Black then add a tiny dot for eye.
3. Add a repetitive pattern to the background.
4. Let paint dry then seal with a satin exterior varnish.

Delta Ceramcoat® Acrylic Paint & Satin Exterior Varnish

Koala Bear

by Kathleen George

What is cute, cuddly and lives in eucalyptus trees? The Koala Bear is only found "down under" in Australia. Like the Kangaroo, it is a marsupial, which means the female carries its young in a pouch. With styrofoam and a mixture of sawdust and paint you can make your own furry Koala bear complete with his own eucalyptus tree.

LEAF PATTERN

You will need:
3" Styrofoam Egg
2" Styrofoam Ball
Two 1" Styrofoam Balls
3½" Styrofoam Wreath
4" x 4" Styrofoam Square
4 Plastic Claws
4.5 mm Plastic Eyes
  with Shanks
6 mm Black Bead
Glue Gel
Green Paper
Gray Acrylic Paint
1 Cup Sawdust
Toothpicks
Plastic Knife
Teaspoon
Craft Snips
Paintbrush
Scissors
Small Branch

1. Cut a slice from the wide end of the styrofoam egg then cut about ½" from the other end. Cut a small slice from one side of the 2" ball. Cut the wreath in half, then each piece in half again. Cut both 1" balls in half.
2. Using toothpicks and glue, attach the ball to the egg with the flat sides together. Flatten one end of each of the four wreath pieces and glue to the body for legs using toothpicks to secure. The curved part should face upwards for the top legs and down for the bottom. Push a plastic claw into the opposite end of each leg facing inward.
3. Shape half of 1" ball to make a nose. Glue to the head using toothpicks Flatten the bottom of two halves of the 1" ball. To make the ears, glue the split balls on each side of the head with the flat part facing front.

4. Sift the sawdust through a large strainer to separate the fine sawdust from the coarse. Set the coarse sawdust aside to use later.
5. Mix 2 - 3 tablespoons cup of gray paint with one cup of fine sawdust. Use your fingers to rub together if necessary to remove any clumps. Spread glue over the surface of the bear then sprinkle with the colored sawdust for "fur". Pat in place gently with your fingers.
6. Glue two eyes into the face on either side of the nose, then glue the black bead onto the nose. Push in place.
7. Glue the small branch to the center of the styrofoam block. Spread glue over the top of the block then sprinkle with coarse sawdust. Snip 1 ½" wide strips of green construction paper to make a fringe then glue around the edge of the styrofoam for grass. Slip the Koala Bear over the branch. Cut green leaves from construction paper then glue to the branch.

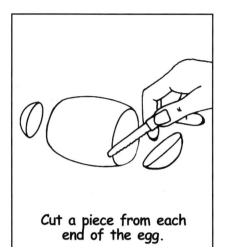

Cut a piece from each
end of the egg.

Cut small piece off one
side of the 2" ball.

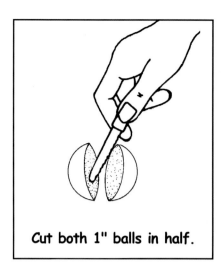

Cut both 1" balls in half.

Cut wreath in half
then in half again.

Glue claws into paws
facing inwards.

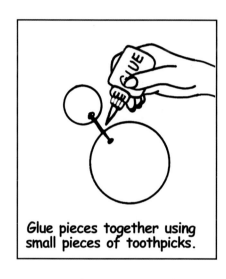

Glue pieces together using
small pieces of toothpicks.

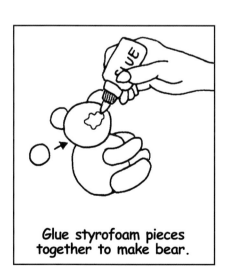

Glue styrofoam pieces
together to make bear.

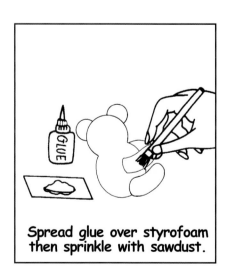

Spread glue over styrofoam
then sprinkle with sawdust.

Fringe green paper then
glue around base.

Darice® Plastic Claws, Eyes & Beads; Delta Ceramcoat® Acrylic Paint;
Dow Styrofoam® Brand Plastic Foam; Elmer's® School Glue Gel; Fiskars® Craft Snips

Woolly Sheep
by Julie McGuffee

You don't have to fall asleep to count millions of sheep if you go to Australia. Sheep farms are an important factor in the Australian economy. In fact one third of the world's wool comes from this continent. You can make just one, or a whole flock!

You will need:
Large Spool $1\frac{1}{2}$" x $2\frac{1}{4}$" - Body
8 Mini Spools $\frac{3}{8}$" x $\frac{1}{2}$" - Legs
Split Egg $1\frac{1}{8}$" x $1\frac{5}{8}$" - Head
75 White $\frac{1}{2}$" Pom Poms
Black Bumpy Chenille
Black Acrylic Paint
2 Small Wiggle Eyes
White Glue
Paintbrush

1. Make four legs by gluing two mini spools together for each leg. Glue to one side of the large spool. Let dry then paint the legs and the split pigeon egg black.

2. Cut a piece of chenille stem with 4 "bumps". Bend each of the outside bumps over to the center of the piece. Twist together to secure then glue to the back of the narrow part of the egg for ears. Cut two chenille bumps. Bend in half then twist ends together. Glue into the hole at one end of the spool for the tail.

3. Cover the spool with glue, except for the end where the head will be glued then cover with pom poms. Stand the spool on its legs, then glue one pom pom directly underneath the hole at the front to support the head. Let dry. Glue the wide part of the head to the pom pom and the top of the head to the edge of the spool as shown in the illustration. Fill in area around the head with pom poms. Glue wiggle eyes to face.

Glue two mini spools together to make legs. Glue to spool.

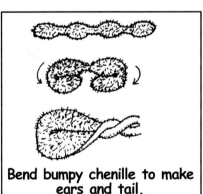

Bend bumpy chenille to make ears and tail.

Glue pom poms all over spool.

Glue one pom pom beneath hole at front to lift head.

Darice® Craftwood, Pom Poms & Chenille Stems;
Delta Ceramcoat® Acrylic Paint; Elmer's® Craft Bond™ Tacky Glue

Join Our Craft Adventure to the
UNITED STATES OF AMERICA

Travel to the 'Melting Pot' of The World and make:

- Native American Jewelry
- Upside Down Doll
- Corn Husk Doll
- Flower Press
- Stencil Lantern • Crazy Quilt

TRIANGLE
PATTERN

Paper Crazy Quilt
by Patty Cox

In the late 1800's, innovative quilters combined silk, rich velvet and brocade patches with a variety of embroidery stitches to create a "Crazy Quilt". This one is made from paper. Ask friends to autograph a patch on your quilt with their name, birthdate and phone number, or a message.

Sample Crazy Quilt Motifs

Cut 7 paper triangles in assorted colors using decorative edge scissors.

You will need:
Construction Paper - Red, Black (2), Purple, Yellow, Orange, Green and Blue
Gold Metallic Fine Tip Marker
Plain and Decorative Scissors
Punches
Glue Stick
Fine Tip Markers
Colored Pencils

1. Cut two 7½" squares from black construction paper. Cut diagonal slits in one square beginning and ending ½" from the edge of the paper. Cut a 6" square from the center of the second 7½" square of black paper to make a frame.

2. Using pattern, cut seven colored triangles from construction paper with decorative edge scissors. Weave colored triangles in and out of the slits in the black paper as shown. Trim ends even with the sides of the paper.

3. To make your quilt look more like patchwork, glue 1" x ¾" squares onto the triangle strips in your quilt. Tuck ends under the black paper.

4. Glue the black frame over the top of the quilt. Trim away excess paper strips at edges. Glue the quilt to the center of an orange piece of construction paper. Cut around the square with the decorative scissors ¼" from the edge. Glue to the center of a purple piece of construction paper, then cut around the quilt ⅜" from the edge.

5. Decorate the top of your crazy quilt with names and birthdays of family members and friends. Draw stitch patterns with markers and colored pencils, or punch small shapes from colored paper and glue to the patches.

6. Tie a bow at the center of a 24" piece of plastic lacing. Tape ends to the back of the quilt.

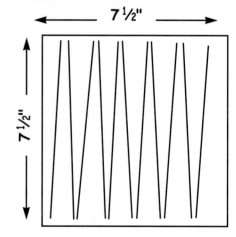

7½"
7½"

Cut diagonal slits in Black paper square.

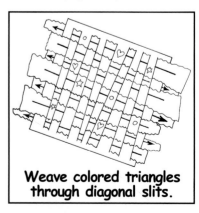

Weave colored triangles through diagonal slits.

Bemiss Jason Construction Paper; Darice® Plastic Lacing;
Fiskars® Paper Edgers & School Scissors, Punches; Elmer's® Craft Bond Paper Glue

Corncrafts

Courtesy of FamilyFun Magazine

Corn husk dolls were introduced to the settlers by the Native Americans. They are easily made from dried corn husks, or the tamale wrappers you find at your local grocery store.

You will need:
Dried Corn Husks
 or Tamale Wrappers
Construction Paper
Colored Markers
String
Glue

1. Soak corn husks in warm water for about 1 hour, or until they become pliable. Tie several damp husks together with a piece of twine about ½" from one end.

2. Hold the bunch by the tied end then fold husks one at a time down over the twine as if you were peeling a banana. Smooth husks over face area then tie together where you want the neck to be.

3. Starting at one long edge, tightly roll a husk for the arms. Wrap twine around each end where the wrists will be.

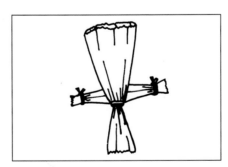

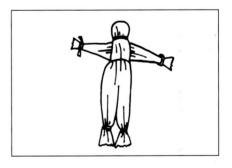

4. Insert the arms between the husks below the head then tie the husks together below the arms to form the doll's waist.

5. To make a skirt, tie more husks around the waist with the longer part up above the dolls head. Secure twine tightly then fold the husks down and smooth the skirt.

6. To make pants, divide the husks below the waist into two bunches. Tie together where the ankles would be. Draw faces on the dolls and dress in paper clothes. Hair can be made from braided twine.

Bemiss-Jason Spectra® Construction Paper;
Elmer's® Craft Bond™ Tacky Glue; Prang® Washable Markers

Upside-Down Doll
by Patty Cox

In Colonial times an Upside-Down doll made from fabric scraps was a favorite toy. Using foam and crêpe paper you can convert your doll from Betsy Ross to Betsy Metallica with just a flick of the wrist.

You will need:

Foam Sheets	Masking Tape
Crêpe Paper Rolls	Cotton Swab
Two Colors Per Doll	Pink Chalk
Glue Stick	Misc. Embellishments:
Glue	Curly Hair, Sequins,
Scissors	Feathers & Pom Poms

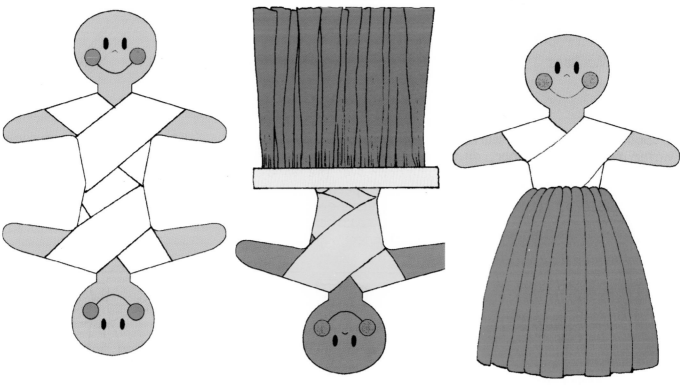

Criss cross crêpe paper around torso to make blouse

Attach strips of crêpe to masking tape to make skirt.

Crêpe paper will cover tape when flipped over.

1. Cut body from foam in selected skin color. Rub cheeks with pink chalk, or powder blush. Draw eyes and mouth with markers.

2. Wrap upper part of body with a 1¾" x 26" strip of crêpe paper. Tape end to back.

3. Cut twenty, 6" strips of crêpe paper. Pinch one end together. Starting ½" from end place crêpe paper strips next to each other on a 5½" piece of masking tape. Wrap tape around the waistline with crêpe paper streamers covering the head. When the doll is held upright, the streamers will fall down to cover the tape. Turn the doll around and repeat process to make a skirt for the other side using different colors of crêpe paper.

4. Glue the hair on head. Decorate doll with hats and accessories. Add motifs to crêpe paper clothing with markers, or embellish with beads, sequins, feathers and glitter paint.

HAT PATTERNS

Slit

Slit

Slit

UPSIDE DOWN
DOLL PATTERN

Cut 1 from
selected skin
color foam

U.S.A.

Bemiss-Jason Crêpe Paper; Dixon Redimark® Markers;
Elmer's Craft Bond Glue Stick, School Glue & Fun Dimensions™ Glitter Gel;
Fiskars® Paper Edgers & Punches; Prang Colored Pencils & Chalk

Stencil Lantern
by Tracia Ledford-Williams

Stenciling on tin is a typical Colonial type craft. Using a tin can we'll make a lantern fit for Paul Revere's midnight ride!

You will need:
Coffee or Soup Can
Wire
Wire Cutters
Needle-Nose Pliers
Scissors
Paintbrushes - Small Round
  and 1" Flat
Glass and Tile Paint - White,
  Navy Blue and Red
Surface Conditioner
Metal Primer
Hammer and Nail
Compressed Sponge
Toothpick

STAR PATTERNS

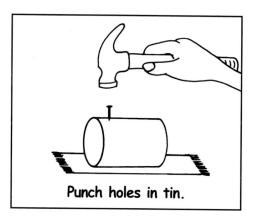

Punch holes in tin.

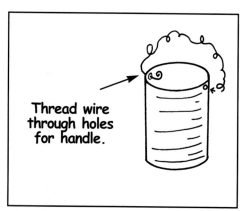

Thread wire through holes for handle.

1. Make a design in the can by punching holes in the sides with a hammer and nail. (It may be easier if you first fill the can with water and allow to freeze.) Place can on a towel to make it easier to hold. Remember to punch holes at the top edge for a handle.

2. Paint the can with surface conditioner. Allow to evaporate then paint with metal primer. Let dry, then basecoat Navy. While the paint is still wet, dip a sponge in Navy then White. Dab paint on the can.

3. Trace star pattern on compressed sponge then cut out. Rinse in water to expand then squeeze out excess water. Dip sponge in Red paint then sponge stars randomly on can. Outline stars with White then add White dots and lines to create starburst design. Use a small round brush to write 'USA' in White on one side. Set aside to dry.

4. Seal paint with clear gloss glaze. Let dry. Thread ends of wire through the holes at the top to make a handle. Bend ends up with pliers.

5. Hammer a nail through the center of the base then place a votive candle over the nail to hold in place.

**Delta Air Dry PermEnamel™, Metal Primer & Surface Conditioner;
Fiskars® Craft Snips, Needle Nose Pliers & Scissors**

Flower Press
by Brenda Spitzer

Wild flowers can be found all over the United States with many varieties blooming in different areas of the country. Using a flower press you can preserve the flowers from your garden, or your neighbor's garden, to make beautiful notecards, bookmarks and stationery.

You will need:
Two 3½" x 5" Rectangular* Plaques
Hand Drill
Four 2½" Bolts
Four Wing Nuts
Wood Sealer
Light Ivory Acrylic Paint
Decoupage Adhesive
Tacky Glue
4 Pieces of Corrugated Cardboard 3½" x 4"
6 Pieces of Newsprint 3½" x 4"
Paintbrush
*Other shapes may also be used.

1. Place wooden plaques together with beveled sides out. Wrap with rubber bands in both directions. Make a mark about ³⁄₈" from corners. Hold, or clamp to a piece of scrap wood on top of your work surface. Drill one hole in each corner where marked then remove clamps and rubber bands.

2. Apply wood sealer to top and sides of both plaques. Let dry completely then apply the sealer to the bottom. Let dry. Sand smooth then remove sanding dust with a damp cloth. Paint plaques Light Ivory.

3. Glue pressed flowers to top of press. When glue is dry, coat with the decoupage sealer. Let the first coat dry then apply a second coat.

4. Assemble press as follows: Place materials you want to press on top of one sheet of newsprint then place the newsprint on top of the cardboard. Place another piece of newsprint on top then a piece of cardboard. Repeat until you have three or four layers. Insert four bolts up through the bottom plaque then place your plant "sandwich" on top of the wood. Place the top of your press over the bolts, press down and secure very tightly with the wing nuts.

5. After four weeks loosen the wing nuts and remove layers. Store the pressed plant material between sheets of newsprint. Use the pressed flowers to decorate notecards or stationery.

Secure plaques with rubber bands.

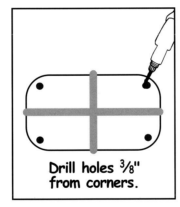

Drill holes ³⁄₈" from corners.

Glue flowers to top then seal.

Make a "Plant Sandwich".

Darice® Wood Plaques; Delta Ceramcoat® Acrylic Paint & Sealer; Elmer's® Craft Bond Matte Finish Decoupage Adhesive; Fiskars® Craft Drill

Native American Jewelry

by Jennie Arthurs

The first inhabitants of the United States provide the inspiration for beautiful beaded jewelry. It's a simple task to make your own using only, beads, cord and safety pins!

You will need:
1 yard of Cord or
  Plastic Lacing
Pony Beads - 40 each of
  Black, White and Turquoise
Seven Turquoise
  Spaghetti Beads
Seven 2" Safety Pins
Spray Sealer

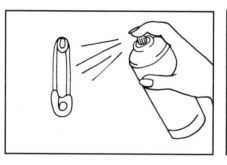

1. Spray safety pins with two thin coats of clear acrylic sealer. This will prevent the silver or brass finish from tarnishing.

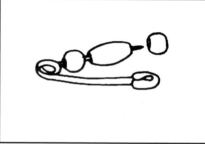

2. Thread the beads onto the safety pins as shown in the illustration.

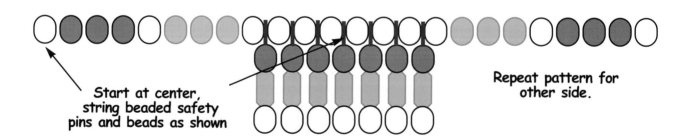

Start at center, string beaded safety pins and beads as shown

Repeat pattern for other side.

3. Assemble necklace by threading the beads and the beaded safety pins onto the lacing. Start at the center point of the necklace and work out to one side, then repeat the pattern on the other side. When the necklace is strung, tie the ends of the cords together in an overhand knot.

Darice® Beads, Cord & Plastic Lacing

Join Our Craft Adventure to
CANADA

On your journey to the North you'll create:

- Walking Stick
- Beat a Leaf Journal
- Totem Pole • Friendship Story Hide
- Nature Stamps

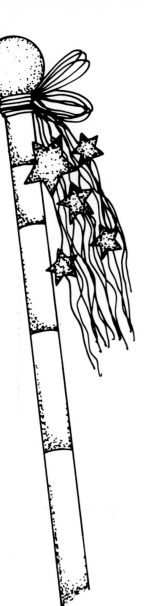

Walking Stick
by Tracia Ledford-Williams

Carry your painted walking stick as you climb Canada's majestic mountains. You can make one from a stick you found in the woods, or you can use a dowel.

You will need:
48" of 1" Dowel
1½" Wood Doll Head
4 Wooden Stars
Craft Drill
Scissors
1" Paintbrush
Acrylic Paint - Purple, Empire Gold, Fuchsia and Green
Exterior Satin Varnish
Wood Glue
Masking Tape

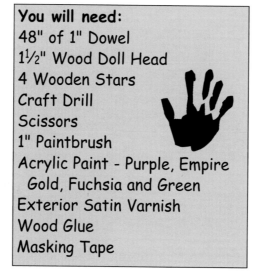

Apply strips of masking tape around dowel.

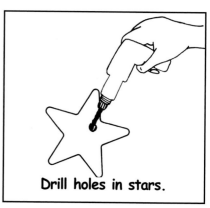

Drill holes in stars.

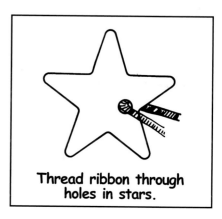

Thread ribbon through holes in stars.

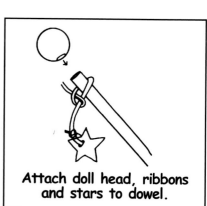

Attach doll head, ribbons and stars to dowel.

1. Apply strips of masking tape around dowel at random intervals. There are 10 different blocks of color on our stick, but you can make as many as you like.

2. Beginning at one end of the stick, paint up to the masking tape with one color. Let dry then remove the tape. Paint a second color up to the next strip of masking tape. Repeat, alternating colors, until all the sections have been painted. Paint the ball Purple.

3. Drill small holes in the stars with the hand drill. Place something on your work surface so that it doesn't become damaged from the drill. Paint the stars Gold.

4. Let the paint dry then seal the stars and stick with 3 coats of varnish. Allow each coat to dry between applications.

5. Glue the ball to the top of the stick. Tie ribbons to the stars, then tie the opposite end of the ribbon to the top of the stick beneath the ball.

Darice® Wood Stars & Doll Head; Delta Ceramcoat® Acrylic Paint & Varnish; Elmer's® Pro Bond™ Wood Glue; Fiskars® Craft Hand Drill

Beat-a-Leaf Journal

Courtesy of FamilyFun Magazine

Nature and the outdoors play an important part in Canada's crafts. We'll use nature's own pigment colors from an assortment of leaves and flowers to create this unique design.

You will need:
Wooden Board
Muslin
Masking Tape
Rock
Assorted Leaves
Pre-Cut Cardboard Mat
Spiral Journal
Glue

1. Select an assortment of leaves then place one leaf on the board. Place a piece of muslin, or other, lightweight fabric on top, taping it down at the corners. Using a rock, carefully beat the fabric over the entire leaf, with consistent and even force. Lift up the fabric and the leaf will have left its image on the inside.

2. To make a journal, glue the leaf printed fabric between a pre-cut cardboard frame, then glue the framed leaf to the cover of an empty book.

3. Try the same technique with different types of flowers to see which varieties work best. You may find that some don't work well at all, but some may give you some beautiful flower print shapes. You can use these to make floral stationery, gift tags and gift bags.

Place a leaf between a board and a piece of muslin.

Pound evenly with a rock.

Frame the patterned muslin then glue to a book cover.

Bemiss-Jason Pre-Cut Mat Frames; Elmer's® Craft Bond™ Tacky Glue

Totem Pole
by Kathleen George

The spirit of *Lekwanmen* is the largest totem pole in the world. It stands in Victoria, British Columbia and took nine months to carve. Your totem pole, a column of animals, is made from styrofoam and small wood pieces and takes less than an hour to make!

You will need:

One 2" Styrofoam Ball	Toothpicks
One 3" Styrofoam Egg	Non-Aerosol Wood Tone
Two 2½" Styrofoam	Spray Paint
Eggs	Acrylic Paint or Markers
Assorted Small	Red, Green and Black
Wood Shapes	Craft Snips
Jumbo Craft Stick	Teaspoon
Glue Gel	Plastic Knife

Create animal heads using styrofoam balls, eggs and small wood shapes. Refer to diagram for placement of small wood shapes. The animals shown are made as follows:

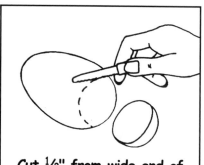

Cut ½" from wide end of egg pieces and flatten top.

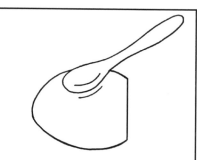

Use a teaspoon to make depressions in styrofoam.

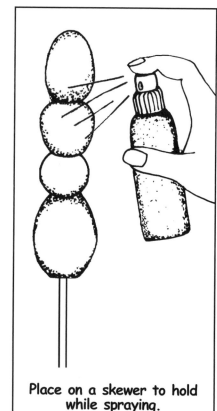

Place on a skewer to hold while spraying.

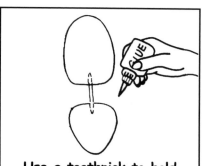

Use a toothpick to hold pieces together when gluing.

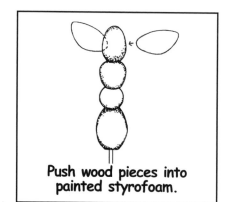

Push wood pieces into painted styrofoam.

Assemble:

1. Glue animals together. Dip a toothpick into glue then push into the top of the bottom animal. Glue the second animal to the top of the first by pushing down over the toothpick. Glue all four animals together in this manner as shown in illustration.
2. Spray the totem pole with several light coats of color mist. *Hint*: Stick a skewer into the base of the totem pole to hold it while you spray.
3. Color the wooden pieces with markers, or paint. Glue to the totem pole to finish as shown.

CANADA

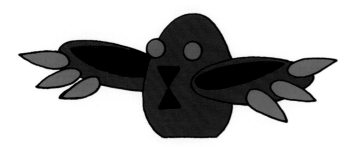

Crow:

Cut a small slice from the wide end of 2½" egg then decorate with small wood pieces:

  Nose - 2 Medium Triangles;
  Eyes - Small Circles;
  Wings - 2 Large Teardrops; 6 Small Teardrops.

Fish:

Cut a small slice from the top and bottom of the 2" styrofoam ball. Decorate with small wood pieces:

  Eyes - 2 Small Circles and 2 Medium Circles;
  Mouth - Large Triangle;
  Fin - Small Oval and Medium Oval;
  Tail - Large Triangle.

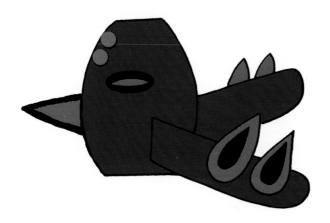

Thunderbird:

1. Cut ½" off the wide end of 3" egg so that it will stand. Cut a small slice from the top.
2. Firmly press a teaspoon into the styrofoam to make grooves for eye sockets.
3. Break a jumbo craft stick in half then push one half into each side of the egg toward the back of the base for wings. These pieces will also help to stabilize your totem pole.
4. Decorate with small wood pieces:
  Eyes - 2 Small Ovals;
  Nose - Large Teardrop;
  Wing Feathers - 4 Medium Teardrops;
  Forehead - 2 Small Circles.

Bear:

1. Cut a small slice from the top and bottom of a 2½" styrofoam egg.
2. Make two shallow dents with your thumbs at the wide of the egg for eye sockets.
3. Compress the bottom front area of the egg with the back of a teaspoon.
4. Decorate with small wood pieces:
  Nose - Medium Circle and Small Circle;
  Eyes - Medium Circles;
  Ears - Medium Circles.

Friendship Story Hide
by Patty Cox

Canada is rich with the tradition of tribal heritage. Tribal stories were often told with pictures, a language rich in design and symbolism. Create a miniature friendship hide to tell your story to share with kindred spirits.

BUFFALO *ABUNDANCE*

BEAR *TRUST*

RABBIT *FEAR*

TURTLE *MOTHER EARTH*

Bear Track	Good Omen
Rattlesnake Jaw	Strength
Butterfly	Everlasting Life or innocence
Rain Clouds	Good Prospects
Lightning	Swiftness
Sun	Happiness
Eagle Feathers	Chief
Cross	Paths Crossing
Thunderbird	Unlimited Happiness
Arrow	Protection
Crossed Arrows	Friendship
Pointing Arrows	Ward off Evil Spirits

You will need:
Tan Construction Paper
Fine Tip Markers
Colored Pencils
Colored Chalk
Glue Stick
Decorative Scissors
Hole Punch
Fabric Stiffener
Cotton Swab
Paper Clips
Paintbrush

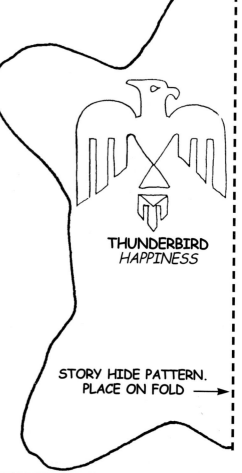

THUNDERBIRD *HAPPINESS*

STORY HIDE PATTERN. PLACE ON FOLD →

1. Fold construction paper in half. Cut out pattern then secure to folded paper with paper clip.

2. Tear the hide shape from the paper following pattern. Draw selected designs around center of hide with markers or colored pencils. Tell a story through your designs.

3. Crumple the paper, then unfold and smooth flat. Rub chalk over the surface. Color the designs then smear chalk with fingers or cotton swab.

7. Apply a generous coat of fabric stiffener with paintbrush. Let dry.

Optional: Glue hide to another color paper. Trim the edges with decorative scissors. Punch a hole in the corner then trim with raffia, beads and feathers.

Bemiss-Jason Spectra Construction Paper; Dixon Redimark® Fine Tip Markers; Elmer's® Craft Bond™ Glue Stick & Fabric Stiffener; Prang® Pastello® Colored Chalk & Colored Pencils

Nature Stamps

by Judi Kauffman for Arts & Crafts Kids Crafts Magazine

Create your own personal set of stamps from wooden blocks and foam shapes. Stamps can be used to personalize all kinds of paper surfaces. You can use these designs or draw some of your own!

1. Trace the stamp patterns onto paper or draw your own. Trace the patterns onto the foam* then cut out.

2. Paint the blocks on all sides. Glue the foam shape to one side of the block. This will be the bottom. Use a marker to draw the same shape on top of the block. It should be in exactly the same position as the foam shape at the bottom.

3. Press stamp on an ink pad then stamp onto paper. Decorate the design with dots and dashes, or simple outlines. Use your stamps to decorate stationery, gift tags, note-cards and more.

*Note: Use one sheet of thick foam, or glue two thin sheets of foam together.

CANADA

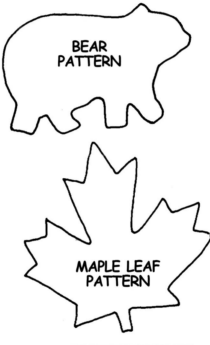

BEAR PATTERN

MAPLE LEAF PATTERN

MOON AND STARS PATTERN

Trace pattern onto foam.

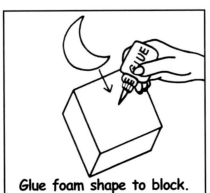

Glue foam shape to block.

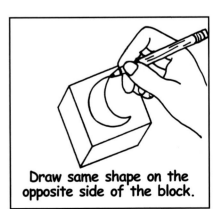

Draw same shape on the opposite side of the block.

Join Our Craft Adventure to
EGYPT, INDIA & MOROCCO

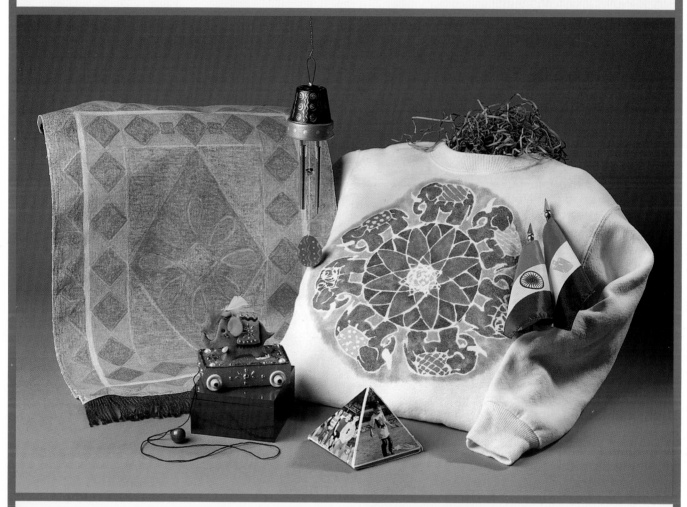

Travel to exotic lands
and make your own:

- Pyramid Pictures • Magic
  Carpet • Wind Chime
- Batik Shirt • Clay Pull Toy

Flag of Egypt

Pyramid Pictures
by Laurie Lazzaro Knowlton

1, 2, 3, 4 pictures all in one place! Display more than one photo at a time with a pyramid shape. Show off your photos the Egyptian way...on a pyramid.

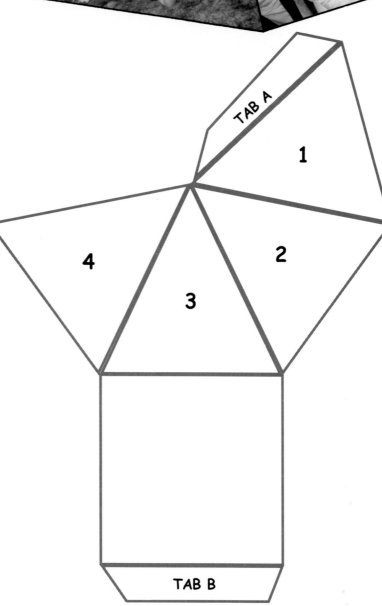

You will need:

Tag Board	Tracing Paper
Paper Glue	Graphite Paper
Scissors	Pencil

Use template to crop photos

1. Trace the pattern then transfer it onto the tag board. This pattern is for 2" triangles built around a 2" square. This size can be increased to accommodate photographs of any size.

2. Cut the pattern out including the tabs.

3. Referring to the illustration, fold on the lines to make the pyramid. Glue Tab A under Section 4. and Tab B under Section 1. Hold together with a rubber band until dry.

4. Trace one triangle pattern then transfer onto the center of a 4" x 4" piece of tag board. Cut out carefully so that you have a square with a triangle cut-out in the center. Use this as a template to place over your photographs, so you can see where the photographs should be cut.

5. Glue photographs to the pyramid then seal with decoupage sealer.

Bemiss-Jason Tag Board;
Elmer's® Acid-Free Craft Bond™ Fabric & Paper Glue and Decoupage Sealer

Batik Shirt

by Kim Thomas

Who can resist the wonderful look of batik... Once a very extensive and messy process, you'll be surprised how easy it has become. Symbolic of India, this shirt is decorated with the lotus flower. Its unfolding petals represent the expansion of the soul and the flower within symbolizes purity and truth. The elephant represents the Hindu God Ganesh, who is the God of wisdom and prosperity.

You will need:
Cotton Ivory Sweatshirt
Shirt Board
Disappearing Marker
Washable Glue Gel
Shirt Board
Fabric Dyes - Fuchsia, Egg
 Yolk Yellow, Turquoise,
 Dark Plum, Leaf Green,
 Robin Blue, Medium Brown
 (3 parts Leather + 1 part
 Lt. Brown)
Tracing Paper
Graphite Paper
Stiff Fabric or Stencil Brush

1. Pre-wash the sweatshirt. **Do not use fabric softener**. Cut templates from cardboard using patterns provided.

2. Place the shirt board inside the shirt then place the double circle template in the center of the shirt front. Trace around it with the marker. Using the circle template, cut another circle from paper. Fold this circle in half, in half again then in half again, always aligning the straight edges. Crease the folds firmly then unfold the paper. It will be divided into eight sections. Place on top of the circle on your sweatshirt and mark each fold line on your sweatshirt circle. Place petal pattern on the circle with the outer tip aligned with the marks on the circle and the opposite end overlapping the center of the circle. Trace petal 8 times. Draw additional petal tips between these petals as shown.

3. Draw the elephants around the outer edge of the circle. They should be evenly spaced with about $1/4$" between tail of one elephant and trunk of the next. Add the pattern for the ear, blanket and the tusk to each elephant. Add a design on the blanket and lines to represent a fringe along the edge.

4. Trace over all the pattern lines with a thin line of glue. Any area that you would like to keep white should also be covered with the glue. Let the glue dry.

5. Paint the shirt with the different colors of fabric dye as shown on the pattern.

6. Let the shirt dry for at least 24 hours then machine wash on a regular cycle with warm water. Repeat until all the glue has washed away to reveal the batik look!

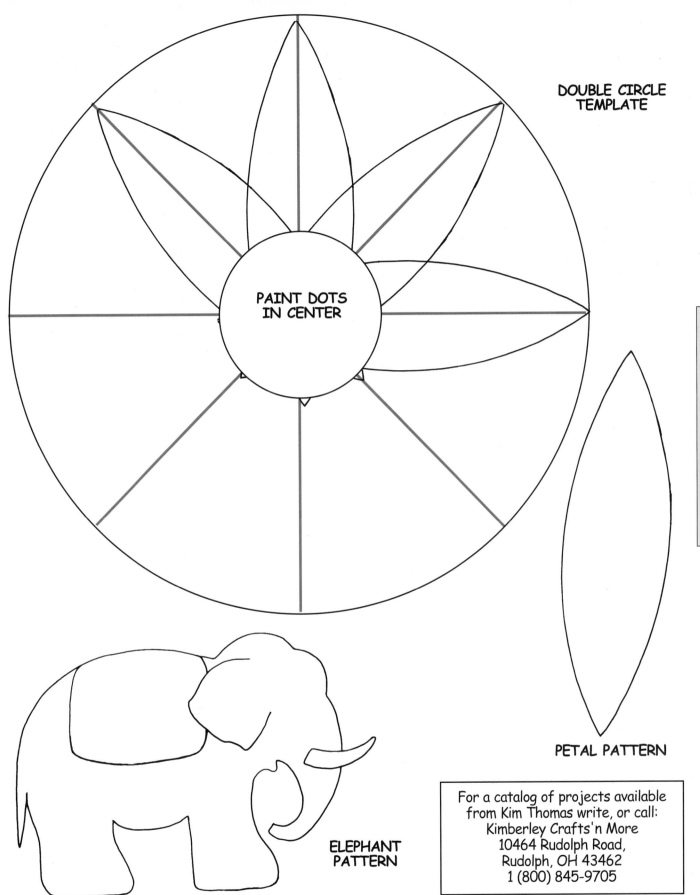

DOUBLE CIRCLE
TEMPLATE

PAINT DOTS
IN CENTER

PETAL PATTERN

ELEPHANT
PATTERN

For a catalog of projects available
from Kim Thomas write, or call:
Kimberley Crafts'n More
10464 Rudolph Road,
Rudolph, OH 43462
1 (800) 845-9705

Delta Brush-On Fabric Dye Color™; Elmer's® School Glue Gel

Wind Chimes
by Tracia Ledford-Williams

From Northern Africa to the Middle East to India, this area of the world is known for its beautiful music with a very different and distinctive sound. Capture the feel of the wind whistling through the desert with your own set of wind chimes.

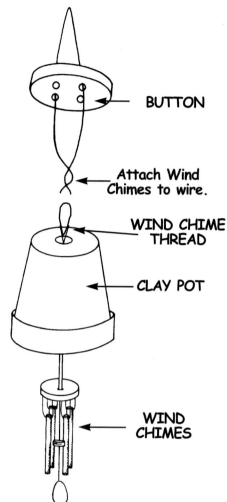

BUTTON

Attach Wind Chimes to wire.

WIND CHIME THREAD

CLAY POT

WIND CHIMES

ASSEMBLY INSTRUCTIONS

You will need:
2" Clay Pot
Set of Chimes
Acrylic Paint - Red, Black, Gold, Copper, Silver
Satin Exterior Varnish
¾" Button
Glue
6" Piece of Wire
Needle Nose Pliers
Paintbrushes

POT PATTERN

1. Paint the base of the pot Black and the rim Opaque Red. Let paint dry then re-paint the rim with Gold.

2. Using a liner brush, paint spirals of Gold, small lines of Silver and wider lines of Copper in a repetitive pattern around the base of the pot. Add Silver dots to the rim.

3. Let dry then seal with satin exterior varnish.

4. Paint the windchimes clapper Opaque Red, then Gold. Paint Silver lines with a liner brush.

5. Bend the wire in half then thread ends through 2 holes in the button. Twist ends together with the pliers.

6. Thread the loop from the top of the wind chime through the hole in the bottom of the pot then attach to the wire. Tie in a knot then secure with a spot of glue. Glue the button to the top of the pot.

Hang in the wind for all to enjoy!

Delta Ceramcoat® Acrylic Paint;
Elmer's® Craft Bond™ Tacky Glue; Fiskars® Needle Nose Pliers

Magic Carpet
by Kathleen George

Some of the world's most beautiful rugs and carpets come from this area of the world, so it's not surprising to hear tales of magic carpets! Climb aboard your own magic carpet, close your eyes and see where it takes you next...

You will need:
16" x 20" White Cotton Duck Fabric
16" x 20" Drawing Paper
Fine Black Permanent Marker
Glue Gel
Crayons
10 yards of Brown Yarn
4 Large Paper Clips
Geometric Patterns
Ruler

Wrap yarn around card, then cut to make fringe.

1. Iron fabric to remove any wrinkles. Squeeze a thin line of glue along the edge to prevent fraying. Set aside to dry.

2. Draw the rug design first on the paper using a dark marker. To mark the center of the paper and the center of each side, fold the paper in half then in half again.

3. Make your design using simple geometric shapes like diamonds, squares and triangles. Use wood shapes for patterns, or cut your own from cardboard. Designs in the Middle East are typically symmetrical with wide borders around a central design. The shapes used usually have straight lines and not a lot of curves. These shapes make up repetitive patterns rather than pictures and the colors used are usually dark with lots of reds and browns.

4. Place the fabric on top of the paper pattern then secure at each corner with large paper clips. Color the design with crayons. Work from left to right (or right to left if you are left-handed) and from top to bottom to avoid smudging something you have already colored. Try to color in the same direction as the weave in the fabric. Use two different colors on top of each other for a very rich and vibrant look.

5. If you plan to wash the rug you will need to heat set the color. Place the fabric, colored side down on a piece of paper then ask an adult to help iron the fabric slowly and carefully with a very hot iron.

6. To make a fringe for the ends, wrap yarn about 50 times around a piece of cardboard about 2½" wide. Cut the loops then remove the cardboard. Cut the yarn in half again. Spread a line of glue gel along the back of the fabric about ¼" from the edge then place the pieces of yarn on the glue to make the fringe.

Dixon Redimark® Permanent Markers; Elmer's® School Glue Gel; Prang® Fun Pro™ Crayons

Clay Pull Toy
by Kathleen George

Children all over the world love toys. Teddy Bears are a favorite here in the United States, but children in India are more likely to play with an elephant because of its importance in Indian life. This little pull-toy features an elephant, but you can use any shape you like. Why not make lots of different animals - you could attach one behind the other to make a circus train!

Color styrofoam with non-aerosol spray paints.

1. Make bread dough recipe by mixing three slices of fresh, crumbled white bread with the crusts removed and one bottle of colored glue. Knead the dough until smooth. Use a rolling pin to roll the dough ½" thick. Use the cookie cutter to cut out elephant (or other animal).

2. Make 2 small balls of dough then flatten into 1" circles for ears. Glue in place.

3. Make half a recipe of dough with a different color glue. Flatten with the rolling pin until it is large enough to cut out a 1" x 3" rectangle. Glue the rectangle to the elephant's back for a blanket. Roll another piece of dough into a ball. Cut in half then glue one half on top of the head for a hat.

4. Press, then glue beads into the blanket to decorate. Add beads for the eyes, cheeks and tusks on the elephant.

5. Push the styrofoam onto a skewer to hold while spraying with red paint. Let dry.

6. Use the axle pegs to make holes in the sides of styrofoam piece ¼" from the bottom and ½" from the end. Place a drop of glue into the holes. Place a wheel on each axle then push the axles into the holes.

7. Decorate the block with decorative glues and beads. Tie a knot at the end of a piece of string. Place a drop of glue on the knot, then push into the end of the styrofoam to secure. Tie a wooden bead onto the opposite end of the string and glue the elephant to the top of the block.

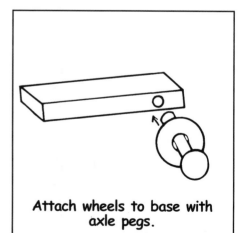

Attach wheels to base with axle pegs.

Join Our Craft Adventure to
MEXICO

Travel 'South of the Border' to make:

- Worry Dolls • Paper Blooms
- Mosaic Bead Pottery
- Fiesta Doll • Pinata Basket

Pinata Basket

by Patty Cox

Pinatas are traditionally made from brightly colored ceramic or papier maché. They are filled with gifts and candy then hung in homes to be broken by children during the Christmas holidays.

You will need:
5 Mesh Plastic Canvas
#16 Tapestry Needle
Pony Beads
Feathers
Straw Satin Raffia
Cord - Natural,
Red, Green, Yellow
and Black

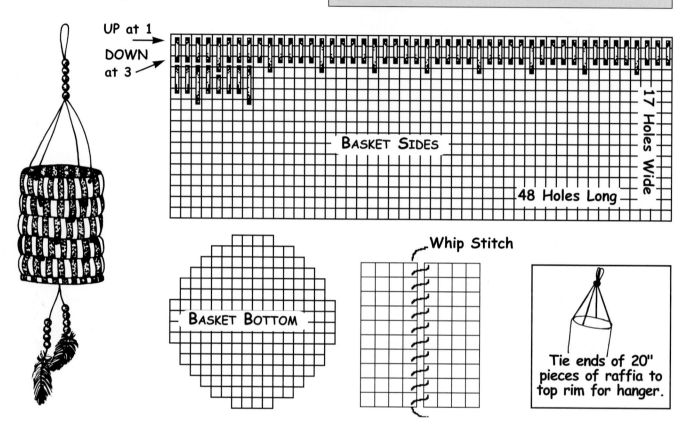

UP at 1
DOWN at 3

BASKET SIDES

17 Holes Wide

48 Holes Long

BASKET BOTTOM

Whip Stitch

Tie ends of 20" pieces of raffia to top rim for hanger.

1. Cut plastic canvas as shown. Thread a needle with a 24" - 36" strand of raffia.

2. Starting at the top left hole, bring raffia up through the back leaving a 2" tail of raffia at the back. Push needle down into the third hole then bring up through the second hole along the top edge. Make three more stitches next to first then on the fifth stitch push the needle down through the fourth hole. Continue making stitches until you have almost reached the end of the raffia. Leave 2" tail at top of the canvas. Thread needle with a different color of raffia. Leaving a 2" tail, continue making stitches with the new color. Tie tail ends together with the knot at the top of the canvas. Clip ends to ½". Completely cover the plastic canvas, alternating colors and lengths of raffia.

3. When the piece of canvas is finished, roll into a tube then whip stitch short edges together. Attach the bottom of the basket to the sides with whip stitches, then whip stitch around the top edge of the basket.

4. Cut two 20" pieces of red raffia. Tie one piece of raffia to top of basket then tie the other end to the opposite side. Tie one end of the second piece to the top edge between the other two ends. Tie the other end to the opposite side. bring cords together and tie with an overhand knot. Thread strands through pony beads. Tie another knot above beads. Tie two 5" strands of raffia to the center of the bottom of the basket. Thread pony beads onto the strands then tie knots beneath the beads to secure. Glue feathers in pony beads.

Darice® Mesh Plastic Canvas, Straw Satin Raffia Cord, Pony Beads & Feathers

Worry Dolls

by Julie Stephani for Great American Crafts Magazine

Chase your cares away with these miniature dolls. All you need are clothespins, craft sticks and pieces of embroidery floss or yarn. You can dress your dolls any way you please!

You will need:

¾" Flat Clothespins
Mini Craft Sticks
Baby Flat Clothespins
Craft Picks
Acrylic Paint - Black and
   Flesh Color
Fine Tip Markers - Black
   and Red
Glue
Scissors
Paintbrush
Craft Snips

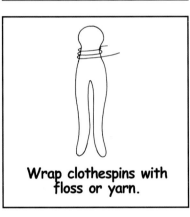

Wrap clothespins with floss or yarn.

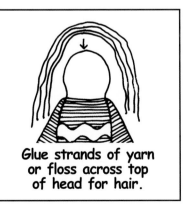

Glue strands of yarn or floss across top of head for hair.

1. To make arms, cut a craft stick in half for large doll and 1" pieces from picks for small doll. Sand any rough edges. Paint arms and clothespin head Flesh. Make small Black dots for eyes and Red dots for cheeks. Paint bottom 1" of clothespins Black for the shoes.

2. Wrap floss around upper body for blouse or shirt. Start at neck and wrap down to waistline. Glue end of floss to secure. For pants, wrap one leg, then beginning at waist wrap floss around hips and down remaining leg. Glue end of floss. To make skirt, start at waist and wrap hips and legs with floss. Change colors to create stripes. Glue rick rack around large girl's waist. Wrap the arms with floss then glue in place.

3. Cut eight lengths of floss for hair. Spread glue over head area then place one strand at a time on glued area. Press in place. Cut hair at neck for the boy doll; trim girls' hair to the desired length.

Option: Use a round doll pin and doll pin base. Paint the base Green to look like grass, or decorate with jewelry, bows and rick rack to personalize your doll.

Darice® Clothespins & Craft Sticks; Delta Ceramcoat® Acrylic Paint; Elmer's® Craft Bond Tacky Glue; Fiskars® Craft Snips

Mosaic Bead Pottery

by Rosanna Gelpi Houck

Pottery is one of Mexico's most beautiful and colorful craft products. We'll start with a clay pot and saucer then we'll add some wonderful beads and grout to make a mosaic design.

You will need:	15 mm Round Cabochons:
6½" Clay Saucer	12 Dark Pink
3½" Clay Pot	12 Pink
Colored Gel	18 Blue
Sponge Brush	18 Green
Glue	18 mm Oval Cabochons:
Acrylic Paint - Light	7 Yellow
Gray and Blue	Tracing Paper
Pencil	Graphite Paper

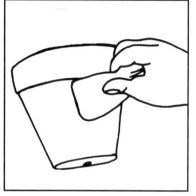

1. Clean the clay pieces with a damp cloth. Let dry.

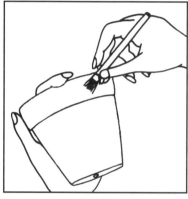

2. Paint center of clay saucer and rim of pot Light Gray. Paint all other areas Blue.

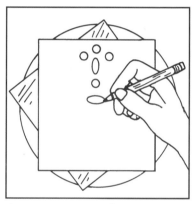

3. Using graphite paper trace pattern lines onto inside of saucer.

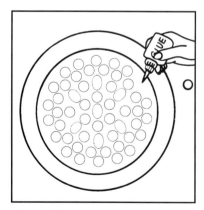

4. Referring to pattern, glue jewels to saucer and pot rim with a dot of glue. Let dry.

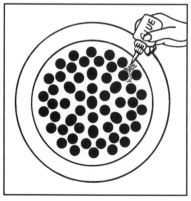

5. Squeeze glue gel around jewels covering all the light grey areas. Let dry thoroughly.

6. Stand pot on its rim then glue the saucer securely to the top.

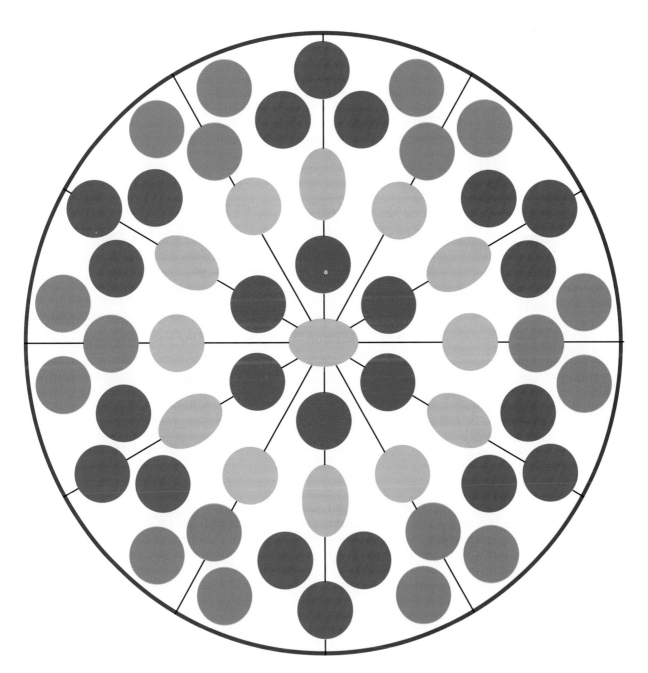

CENTER OF SAUCER PATTERN

POT RIM PATTERN

Delta Ceramcoat® Acrylic Paint;
Elmer's® Fun Dimensions™ Cool Gel; Darice® Cabochons

Fiesta Doll

by Julie Stephani for Great American Crafts Magazine

Vibrant colors play an important part in Mexican designs. This festive doll made from a styrofoam base looks as if she's ready to dance!

You will need:

4" x 9" Styrofoam Cone	Powder Blush
2½" Styrofoam Ball	Two 12" Tan Chenille Stems
⅛ yard each of 5 Brightly Colored Fabrics	4" x 4" Tan Felt
	Small Basket
⅛ yard of White Fabric	Paper Shreds
12" of ⅛" Ribbon - Purple, Gold and Orange	Mini Vegetables
	Fabric Glue
Mini Craft Stick	Pinking Shears
Nylon Hosiery	Knife
4 ply Yarn - Black	Scissors
2 Round 6mm Black Beads	Glue

1. Glue a toothpick into the styrofoam ball. Cut a 3" piece from the leg of nylon hosiery. Gather one end and tie tightly with string. Turn inside-out and pull over the styrofoam ball. Gather around the toothpick at base of ball then tie tightly with string. Cut 1" from the top of the cone then glue the toothpick into the cone.

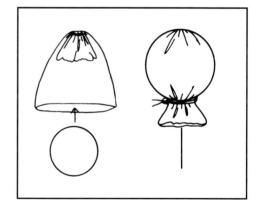

2. Glue two black beads to the front of ball for eyes. Push firmly into the foam. Brush cheeks with powder blush.

3. To make hair, cut fifty 24" lengths of yarn and tie together in the center. Spread glue over the head. Arrange hair on the head and pull to one side in a ponytail. Tie together, separate tails into three equal bundles then braid. Tie strands together 1" from end. Trim ends.

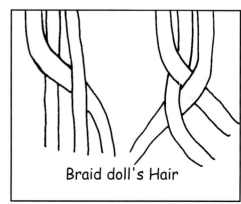

Braid doll's Hair

4. For each arm, cut 3" off each chenille stem. Fold in half and twist together. Cut four felt arms. Glue two arms together on either side of chenille stem.

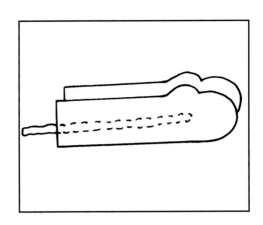

ARM PATTERN
CUT 4

5. Cut two 4" x 6" pieces of white fabric for sleeves. Overlap short ends and glue to form a tube. Pull one sleeve over each arm. Gather top of sleeve then tie tightly at top of arm. Gather the bottom of the sleeve just above elbow then tie tightly. Bend chenille above arm, cover with glue and insert into cone just below the head.

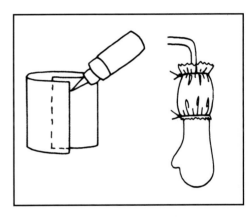

MEXICO

6. To make skirt and blouse, cut colored fabric into $1\frac{1}{2}$" squares with decorative scissors. Insert pencil point into the center of the wrong side of each square. Apply glue to point of fabric. Starting $\frac{1}{2}$" from base of cone, push fabric squares $\frac{1}{2}$" apart into styrofoam with pencil point. Start with a row of white for petticoat then complete covering cone with a variety of colors. Use white fabric at top for blouse.

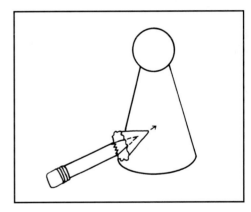

7. Glue flowers across top of hair. Push six white squares into the head in a line behind the flowers. Tie purple ribbon in a bow and glue to the top of the blouse at the center. Glue two ribbon lengths of each color under the last flower of headband. Wrap ribbon around braid then tie at end. Fill the basket with paper crinkles. Place mini vegetables on top then glue hands to basket handle.

Dow Styrofoam® Brand Plastic Foam;
Elmer's Craft Bond Fabric Glue; Fiskars® Pinking Shears

Paper Blooms
by Rosanna Gelpi Houck

In Mexico tissue paper flowers are everywhere. Sold on every street corner they are decorating homes with a rainbow of vibrant colors. They are so festive and bright you'd almost think they were real!

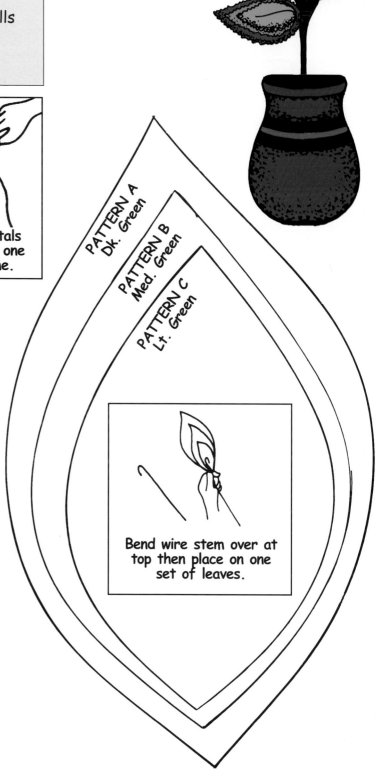

You will need:
Colored Tissue Paper -
  4 Colors per Flower,
  Dk. Green, Med.
  Green, Lt. Green
2" Styrofoam Balls
Floral Tape
18" Wire Stems
Glue

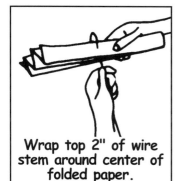

Wrap top 2" of wire stem around center of folded paper.

Gently fan petals apart lifting up one layer at a time.

1. Select tissue paper for petals then cut each sheet into four, 10" x 15" pieces. Make two sets of tissue sheets with two sheets of each color in each set.

2. Cut the long edges of tissue paper with decorative scissors then stack tissue pieces together with darkest color on the bottom and the lightest color on top.

3. Make 1" wide accordion pleats in each set of tissue paper. With the color for center petals on top then wrap top 2" of wire stem around center to secure.

4. Gently fan the petals, lifting up each top petal, one at a time, until the flower is complete.

5. Cut styrofoam ball in half then cover the rounded half with a 6" square of White or Yellow tissue paper. Glue excess tissue to the flat side of the ball then glue ball to center of the flower.

6. Beginning at base of flower, wrap stem with floral tape.

7. To make leaves, cut three each from patterns A, B and C. Assemble groups of leaves with the small one on top and the large one on the bottom. Bend top 1" of a wire stem over then place on one set of leaves. Attach leaves to the wire with floral tape.

PATTERN A
Dk. Green

PATTERN B
Med. Green

PATTERN C
Lt. Green

Bend wire stem over at top then place on one set of leaves.

Bemiss-Jason Tissue Paper; Fiskars® Paper Edgers

Join Our Craft Adventure to
ITALY

Create these colorful and fun Italian crafts:

- Stained Glass Suncatchers
- Mosaic Tile
- Crayon Resist Pot
- Cathedral Window
- Glow in the Dark Glass

Mosaic Tile

by Cecille Diez

Known for its beautiful paintings, Italy's artwork is not confined to just canvases. Walls and floors are covered with intricate mosaic designs and pictures. Create this same mosaic look for a decorative piece for your own home using leftover tile and markers.

You will need:	Ruler
Permanent Markers	Glue
12" x 12" Tile	Picture Hanger

1. Select a tile for your design.
2. Choose an authentic tile pattern, or create your own design.
3. Sketch the pattern onto the surface of the tile using a pencil and a ruler.
4. Draw over your design with a variety of colors of permanent markers. Allow the surface to dry thoroughly.
5. Attach a picture hanger to the back if desired.

Dixon Redimark® Permanent Markers; Elmer's® Craft Bond™ Tacky Glue

Cathedral Window

by Patty Cox

This glittering "stained glass" window also glows in the dark!

You will need:
Non-Bleeding Tissue
  Paper - White, Light
  Blue, Apple Green,
  Purple and Turquoise
Iridescent Chenille Stems
Decorative Scissors
6" Metal Ring
Glue Gel
Glow Glue
Flat Paint Brush
12" x 12" Wax Paper
Prism

1. Cut a 6" square from each color of tissue. Set White aside. Fold other colors in half then in half again then fold the 3" square as shown at right.

2. Place each folded piece on work surface as shown on diagram. Hold points in place with masking tape. Cut out small pattern from card then place over the pieces of tissue paper aligning the straight edge. Cut along arc with decorative scissors. Remove tape then gently open out each piece of tissue. Press creases flat.

3. Squirt equal parts of glow gel and glitter gel onto wax paper. Mix together then paint over a 6" square area in the center of the wax paper. Place the White tissue over this area, then brush surface with glue mixture. Starting with the colored tissue with the smallest hole, layer the colored squares of tissue on top of the White, brushing each layer with the glue mix. Let dry.

4. Wrap the chenille stems around the ring. Use a small piece of the chenille to make a hanger at one side of ring. Slide a prism onto another piece of the chenille and attach to opposite side. Add a bow to hanger if desired.

5. Squeeze a line of glue along one side of the chenille ring then center on top of the tissue layers. Allow to dry then trim away excess tissue.

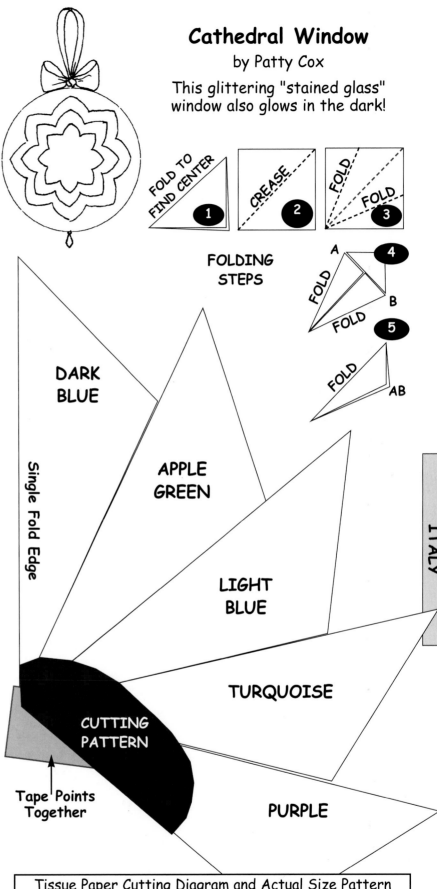

FOLDING STEPS

1 FOLD TO FIND CENTER
2 CREASE
3 FOLD / FOLD
4 A / FOLD / FOLD / B
5 FOLD / AB

DARK BLUE

APPLE GREEN

LIGHT BLUE

TURQUOISE

PURPLE

ITALY

Single Fold Edge

CUTTING PATTERN

Tape Points Together

Tissue Paper Cutting Diagram and Actual Size Pattern
Place Folded Tissue On Diagram and Tape in Place.

Bemiss-Jason Kolorfast® Tissue;
Elmer's® Fun Dimensions™ Ice-A-Delic™ Cool Gel & Glow Gel

Crayon "Resist" Pot
by Brenda Spitzer

You'll be surprised how many elements of Italian art can be found in this one small project. From the use of pottery to the resist technique, your work will be nothing short of magic!

You will need:
4" Terra Cotta Pot
Sealer
Matte Varnish
Acrylic Paint - White and Red
Crayons - Lt. Blue, Yellow and
  Lt. Green
Red Neon Glue
Glow Glue - Yellow and Orange
Flat Brush
Sponge

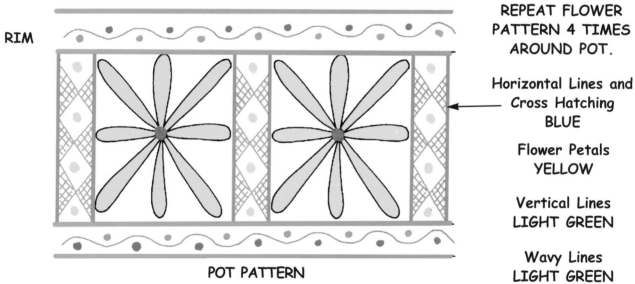

RIM

POT PATTERN

REPEAT FLOWER
PATTERN 4 TIMES
AROUND POT.

Horizontal Lines and
Cross Hatching
BLUE

Flower Petals
YELLOW

Vertical Lines
LIGHT GREEN

Wavy Lines
LIGHT GREEN

1. Paint the inside and outside of the pot with a mixture of one part white acrylic paint to one part sealer.

2. Use crayons to make designs around the pot as shown in illustration.

3. Using a damp sea sponge, wipe Cardinal Red paint around the sides of the pot. Allow to dry. Rinse sponge then use to gently buff the sides of the pot until the crayon shows through. Dried paint will not stick to crayon because the soybean oil in the crayon 'resists' the paint. Seal the pot with a coat of matte varnish.

4. Add orange glow glue and red neon glue gel dots above and below wavy lines. Add red neon gel dots to center of the flowers and yellow glow glue dots between cross-hatching.

Delta Ceramcoat® Acrylic Paint, Sealer & Matte Varnish; Prang Fun Pro™ Crayons;
Elmer's® Fun Dimensions™ Funk-A-Delic Neon Gel & Glow Creations™

Stained Glass Suncatcher
by Tracia Ledford-Williams

Italy is the home of the Pope. He lives in the Vatican City which is in the center of Rome. This has had a great influence on religious art in Italy. The many cathedrals have also made stained glass an important part of Italian art history which is the inspiration for these wonderful suncatchers.

You will need:
Pre-Drilled Glass Shapes
Glass and Tile Paint - Blue Ice, Orange Tango, Purple Pizazz, Emerald Green, Golden Glow and Raspberry Sherbert
Surface Conditioner
Gloss Glaze
Gold Renaissance Foil
Dimensional Foiling Adhesive
Gold Ribbon

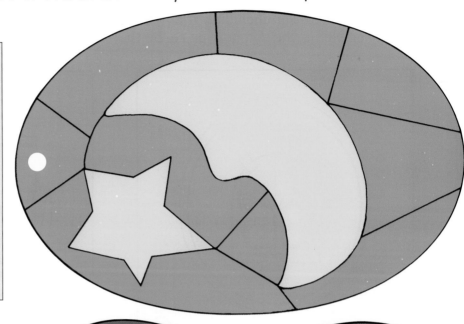

1. Lay the glass shapes on top of the pattern. Trace the design with dimensional adhesive. Allow to dry until it is tacky to the touch.

2. Lay gold foil with the gold, shiny side up, on top of the adhesive. Rub over foil with your finger or a soft toothbrush. The gold will stick to the adhesive. Fill in the patterns with shimmering glass and tile paint.

3. When dry, brush gloss glaze over painted surface to finish. Allow to dry completely. Thread ribbons through holes then knot the ends together to make hanger.

Delta PermEnamel™ Glass & Tile Paint, Gloss Glaze & Surface Conditioner, Renaissance Foil and Adhesive

Glow in the Dark Glass

by Laurie Lazzaro Knowlton

Many designs are symbolic. They are incorporated in many different mediums including stained glass. The butterfly, for example, is the symbol for re-birth.

1. Tape pattern onto a cookie sheet.

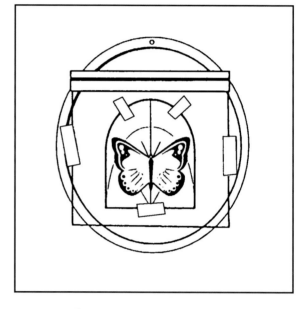

2. Tape large, clear plastic storage bag over the pattern on the cookie sheet.

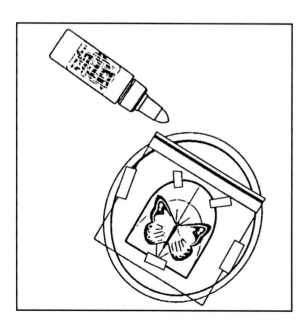

3. Color in the open areas of pattern on the plastic with colored glue. Be sure to fill areas as evenly as possible.

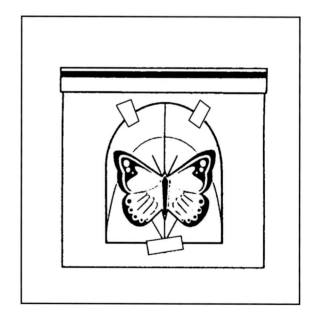

4. Let dry 24 hours or until color looks consistent. Peel off plastic and hang on a smooth surface. The glass will glow in the dark after exposure to light.

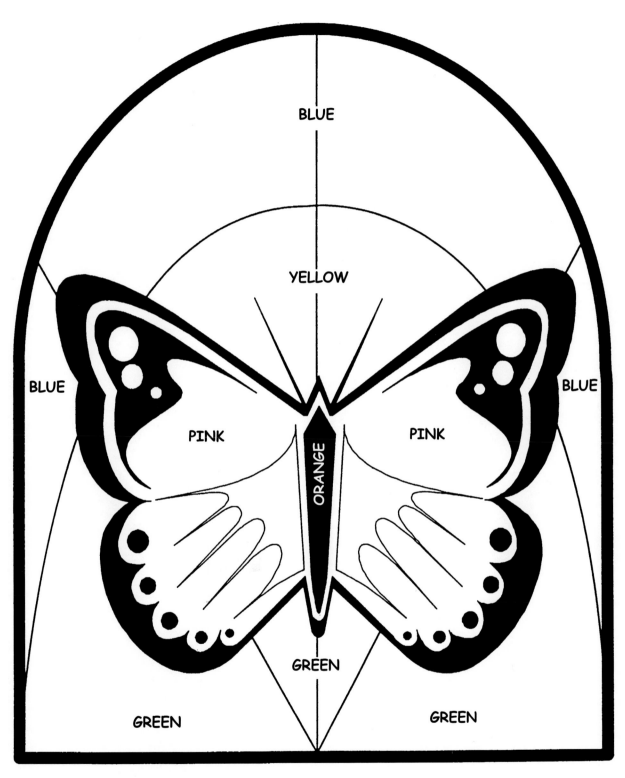

Outline with Dark Blue glue then fill in areas with colors indicated or choose your own colors.

Join Our Craft Adventure to
AFRICA'S Animal Kingdom

While on Safari, we'll learn to make these fun crafts:

- T-Shirt Snake • Baby Hippo
- Wild Animal Puppets
- Paper Chain Animals
- Photo Page - 'It's A Jungle Out There' • Lizard Shirt

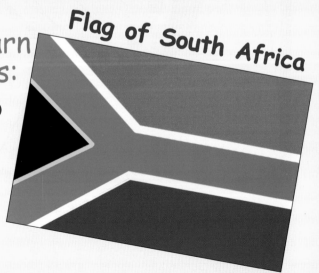

Flag of South Africa

T-Shirt Snake

Courtesy of FamilyFun Magazine

When is a snake not a snake - when it loosens up and becomes a T-Shirt! A visit to Africa would not be complete without going on a Safari to see the animals. Make yourself a fun T-Shirt to wear as you snake your way through the jungle. This design will make you feel right at home.

You will need:
Prewashed T-Shirt
21" Length of 16-gauge
  Floral Wire
Pliers
Twist Ties
Heavy Duty Thread
Needle
Fabric Paints, or Non-
  Aerosol Spray Paint
Paintbrushes

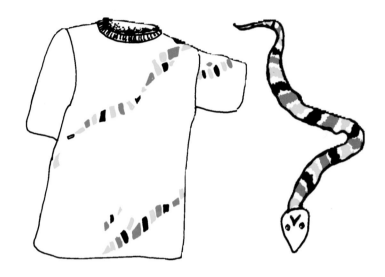

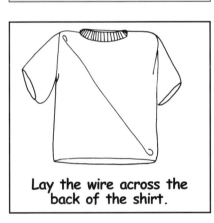

Lay the wire across the back of the shirt.

Scrunch the shirt around the wire. Secure with twist ties then wrap with thread.

1. Lay the shirt front side down. Use the pliers to bend back the sharp ends of the wire. Then, place the wire diagonally on the shirt back, with one end on the left sleeve and the other end touching the lower right corner.

2. Form the snake's head by folding the corner of the sleeve over the end of the wire. Then, fold over the sides of the sleeve and secure with a twist tie. Cover and secure other end of the wire with the bottom of the shirt in the same manner. This becomes the snake's tail. Scrunch the rest of the shirt around the wire, applying a twist tie every few inches to hold in place.

3. Insert a threaded needle into a fold near the base of the head, then wrap the thread firmly around the snake's body starting at the base of the head and winding your way down to the tip of the tip of the tail. Remove the twist ties as you reach them. Knot and trim thread at the end.

4. Color the snake with bright fabric paints. Let dry. When you are ready to wear your shirt, snip the thread, remove the wire and open up the shirt. The snake design will repeat down the shirt. Heat-set the paint according to manufacturer's directions.

ANIMAL KINGDOM

For more T-shirt surprises, see "McCall's Creates" booklet No. 14220 available at fabric stores.

Bemiss-Jason Art Fun™ Twists; Delta Brush-On Fabric Paint; Fiskars® Needle Nose Pliers

Baby Hippo

by Kathleen George

It is unbelievable how much a hippopotamus' mouth can actually hold. Our smaller version has a secret compartment you can fill with surprises.

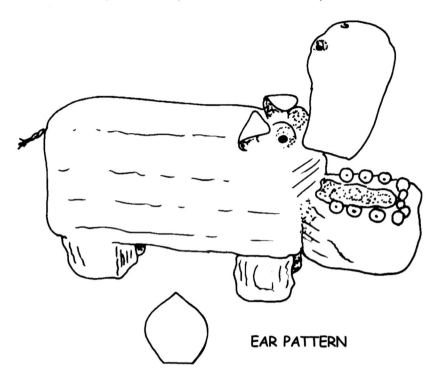

EAR PATTERN

You will need:
2" x 2" x 6" Styrofoam Block
Four 1" Styrofoam Balls
Two $^3/_8$" Beads
Two 8mm Beads
Glue Gel
Tissue Paper - Buttercup
 Luster and Red
1" Flat Brush
White "E" Beads
4" Brown Yarn
Scissors
Pencil
Plastic Knife
Teaspoon
Black Permanent Marker

1. Using the blunt edge of a plastic knife, make a shallow groove around the block, about 2" from the end.

2. Shave $^1/_4$" - $^1/_2$" off the edges of the block, then smooth and round the edges with the back of the teaspoon.

3. Compress and smooth all the edges of the mouth section with your fingertips. The top of the mouth should be pressed firmly in center to define the nostril areas. Shape the bottom of the mouth into a gentle curve.

4. Cut off the top half of the mouth. Begin by cutting down about $^1/_2$" along the groove, then cut in about $^1/_2$" all around the sides. If the mouth does not pop off with the first cuts, go around again and cut a little deeper.

5. Gently scoop a shallow hole out of the inside of the top and bottom parts of the mouth with the teaspoon. Smooth with your fingertips.

6. Make fat, little legs by flattening 1" balls into a square against a hard surface. Glue to the bottom of hippo. Let glue dry thoroughly.

7. Glue large beads into the block just behind the mouth for eyes and smaller beads into the nostril areas.

8. Tear tissue paper into rectangles that roughly cover the major parts of the hippo's body. Tear 3" x 3" squares to cover each leg.

9. Squeeze gel onto tissue paper then spread over the entire surface with a wide brush. Center a small square over a leg, then use a clean soft brush to gently stroke the tissue down over the sides of the leg. Cover each leg in the same manner, then cover the hippo with the larger pieces of tissue. Smooth the tissue over the eyes and nostrils. Glue two pieces of tissue together. Let dry then cut out the ears. Use a pencil point to make holes at the top of the head for the ears, then glue the ears into the holes.

10. Glue a small piece of red tissue to the inside top and bottom of the mouth. Glue the top part of the mouth in place with a piece of tissue as a hinge.

11. Press "E" beads in place around the edge of the upper and lower jaw then glue in place to secure. Use a permanent marker to draw the eyes and nostrils. Use a pencil to make a hole in the back of hippo. Glue 1" piece of yarn in the hole for the tail.

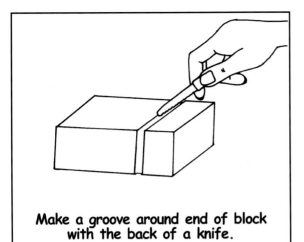

Make a groove around end of block
with the back of a knife.

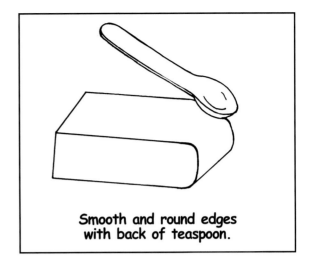

Smooth and round edges
with back of teaspoon.

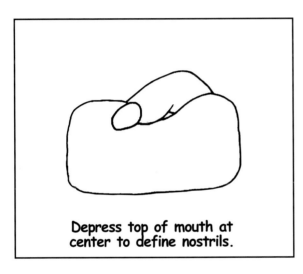

Depress top of mouth at
center to define nostrils.

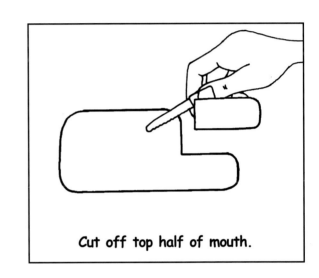

Cut off top half of mouth.

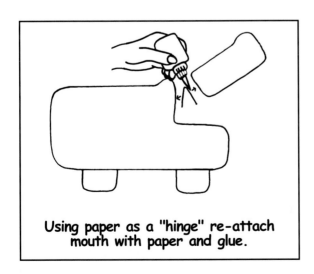

Using paper as a "hinge" re-attach
mouth with paper and glue.

Spread glue over tissue paper then
place on hippo.

**Bemiss-Jason Tissue Paper; Dow Styrofoam® Brand Plastic Foam;
Elmer's® School Glue Gel; Fiskars® Student Scissors**

"Wild" Animal Puppets
by Kathleen George

If animals could only talk, can you imagine the tales they'd have to tell! Make up your own animal stories through these wild and whimsical animal puppets. Your tales can be as crazy as the puppets themselves.

You will need:
4" Styrofoam Egg
1½" Styrofoam Ball
Acrylic Paint
Paintbrush
Chenille Stem
15mm Wiggle Eyes
Glue
Glitter Glue
Assorted Embellishments:
 Twist Ties,
 Chenille Stems, Felt,
 Fuzzi Felt, Yarn, Pom
 Poms, Beads and
 Feathers, etc.

1. Cut the ball in half and the egg in half lengthwise.

2. Glue the split balls onto the rounded part of the egg for the eyes. Different looks can be achieved by placing the eyes in different areas. Let the glue dry.

3. Paint the puppet a bright color.

4. Glue wiggle eyes onto the eyeballs. Cut a chenille stem in half. Bend each into a "U" shape then push the chenille ends into the bottom of the puppet.

5. Decorate your puppet to make it look as wild and crazy as possible using feathers, felt, additional styrofoam balls and other embellishments.

Tips:
1. Place the puppet on a skewer to hold while painting, then place the skewer in a glass until the paint is dry.

2. Use straight pins to hold items in place while glue dries.

3. Make a hole in the styrofoam with pencil point. Put a drop of glue in the hole before inserting material to be glued.

4. To glue yarn, cover the end with glue then push into the styrofoam with a wooden skewer.

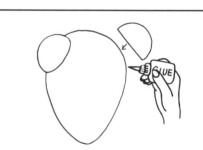

Glue both halves of the ball to the egg for eyes.

Bend 6" piece of chenille into "U" shape. Glue ends into the bottom of the egg.

Darice® Assorted Embellishments;Delta Ceramcoat® Acrylic Paint; Dow Styrofoam® Brand Plastic Foam; Elmer's® Craft bond™ Tacky Glue & Fun Dimensions™ Glitter Gel

Lizard Shirt and Cap

by Tracia Ledford-Williams

When we talk about Africa, we automatically think of the jungle. However, the landscape varies greatly. Almost one third of the African continent is desert, one half is savannah and only the remainder, the smallest part is claimed by the rainforest.

You will need:
Beige T-Shirt and/or Cap
Compressed Sponge
Shimmering Fabric Paint -
  Yellow, Violet, Green and Blue
Fine Tip Black Permanent Marker
Paintbrushes
Scissors
New Pencil with Eraser

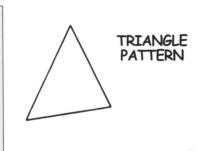

TRIANGLE PATTERN

DRAGONFLY PATTERN

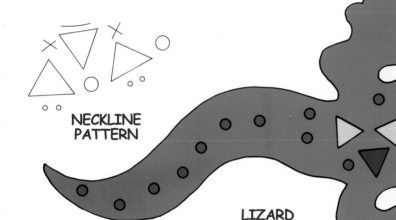

NECKLINE PATTERN

LIZARD PATTERN

1. Place a cardboard form inside a pre-washed T-Shirt over. *Hint:* Do not use fabric softener.

2. Trace then transfer the pattern onto the shirt, or cut around the pattern, place on the shirt and draw around it with a black pen.

3. Trace triangle pattern onto compressed sponge. Cut out shape then dip the sponge in clean water to expand. Squeeze out excess water.

4. Paint the lizard Green. Let the paint dry. Paint Blue and Yellow triangles and Blue dots on his back. Paint the firefly's wings Violet (large) and Blue (small). Paint a trail of Blue dots behind the firefly.

5. Dip the sponge into Violet then use to paint triangles around the T-Shirt neck. Add Yellow triangles in the same manner. Paint the 'X's Green then use the pencil eraser to make Blue dots. Use a toothpick to make the small dots. The cap is painted in the same manner.

6. Let the paint dry thoroughly then place in a dryer for 20 minutes to heat set the paint. Wait four days before laundering, then wash inside-out as necessary.

Delta Starlite Shimmering™ Fabric Color;
Dixon Redimark® Fine Tip Marker; Fiskars® Student Scissors

It's a Jungle Out There
by Fiskars, Inc.

Picture yourself on safari. You're travelling across a broad plain where herds of giraffes and zebras graze in the distance. Your senses are alert to the constant danger - lions or tigers could pounce at any moment. Suddenly a tiger pounces and the animals scatter. Guess where they turned up? Right in the middle of your scrapbook! What a fun scrapbook page this is. See how many other animals you can make in this manner.

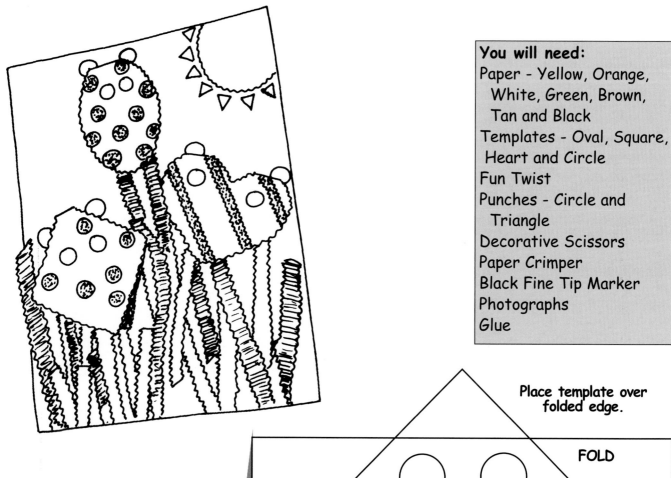

You will need:
Paper - Yellow, Orange,
 White, Green, Brown,
 Tan and Black
Templates - Oval, Square,
 Heart and Circle
Fun Twist
Punches - Circle and
 Triangle
Decorative Scissors
Paper Crimper
Black Fine Tip Marker
Photographs
Glue

Tiger:

Fold yellow paper in half. Use a square stencil to trace shape onto paper as shown. Cut along pattern line with Ripple scissors. Punch two holes for eyes. Punch seven circles from black paper then glue to the tiger. Glue two punched circles behind the fold for ears.

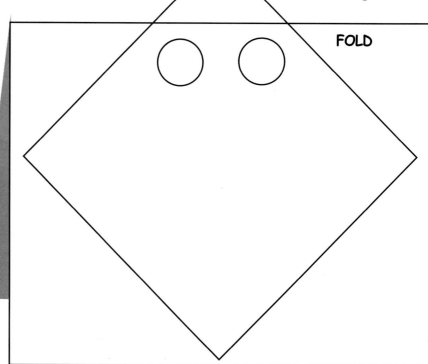

Place template over folded edge.

FOLD

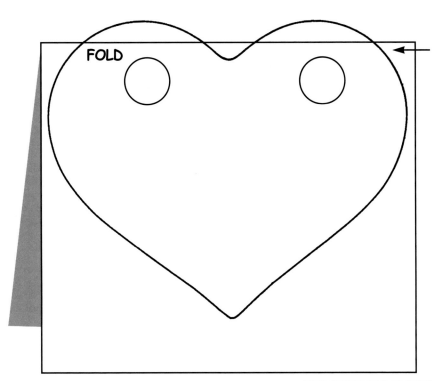

FOLD

Place template over folded edge.

Zebra:

Fold white paper in half. Use a heart stencil to trace shape onto paper as shown. Cut out with Peeks scissors. Punch two holes for eyes. Cut three narrow strips of black paper with Ripple scissors then glue to the Zebra. Glue two punched circles behind the fold for ears.

Place template over folded edge. ➝

FOLD

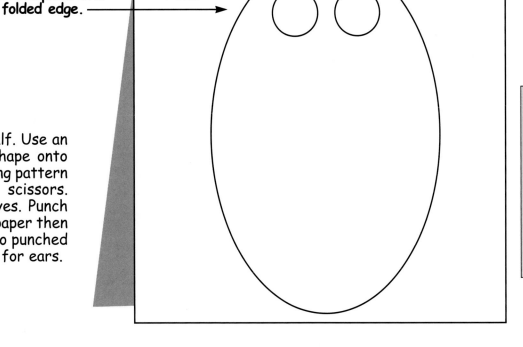

Giraffe:

Fold orange paper in half. Use an oval stencil to trace shape onto paper as shown. Cut along pattern line with Dragonback scissors. Punch two holes for eyes. Punch ten circles from black paper then glue to giraffe. Glue two punched circles behind the fold for ears.

Sun:

Use the stencil to draw a circle on yellow paper. Cut out with deckle scissors. Glue to the upper corner of the blue background paper with part of the sun over the edge. Cut off the excess. Punch four orange triangles and three yellow triangles. Glue around the sun.

Assemble: Crop your photograph so that your eyes peek through the animal's eyes. Glue in place inside the folded paper. Arrange the giraffe, tiger and zebra on the paper, then glue in place. Cut a variety of sizes of green, brown and tan paper strips for grass. Feed through the crimper then glue along the bottom of the page for grass. Fun twists can also be crimped then glued beneath the animals for legs. Use the sun shape to write a short paragraph about what happened.

Bemiss-Jason Spectra® Fadeless™ Paper & Fun Twists; Elmer's Craft Bond™ Fabric & Paper Glue; Fiskars® Decorative Stencils, Paper Crimper, Paper Edgers & Punches

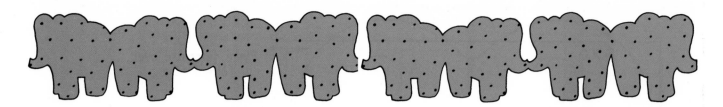

Paper Chain Animals
by Julie McGuffee

Create a whole herd of animals with just a few snips of the scissors. Join two or more together and in no time at all you'll be surrounded by animals, in every shape and color!

You will need:
Brush Markers
Tracing Paper
Graphite Paper
Assorted 8½" x 11" Paper
Honeycomb Paper
Cardstock
Pencil
Scissors
2" Green Pom Pom
2 Wiggle Eyes

TIGER PATTERN

ELEPHANT PATTERN

Fold each piece into four, accordion style. Place pattern on folded paper.

1. Trace each animal onto tracing paper then transfer each pattern onto cardstock. Cut the shapes out.

2. Make patterned paper by coloring the paper all over with markers.

3. Fold the paper in half lengthwise then cut along the fold. Fold each piece in half, then in half again. Place the pattern onto the folded paper so that it overlaps a little at each side then draw around the pattern with a pencil. Cut out through all four thicknesses of paper.

4. Unfold the paper to reveal your paper chain! You can make lots of paper chains in this manner using a variety of papers, or by coloring plain paper with markers or crayons.

Honeycomb Snake
Cut 2" circles from different colors of honeycomb paper. The more circles you cut, the longer your snake will be. Make sure that the lines in the circles are running in the same direction, then glue one circle on top of another until all of them are glued together. Glue a large green pom pom on top of the last circle, then glue two wiggle eyes to the pom pom. Let glue dry then pick up your snake and watch him grow!

Bemiss-Jason Honeycomb Paper; Elmer's® School Glue Gel;
Fiskars® Student Scissors; Prang® Crayons & Washable Markers™

Join Our Craft Adventure to
AFRICA

Create these crafts on your African journey:
- Dance Mask • Shekere
- Kwanza Beads • Floor Cloth
- Mancala Game

Flag of Central African Republic

Floor Cloth
by Tracia Ledford-Williams

Design and color is one of the most important elements of African design. Transform a piece of left-over floor covering into a beautiful floor cloth using acrylic paints!

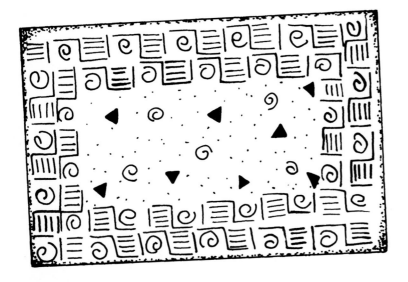

You will need:
Piece of Leftover Vinyl Floor Covering (about 17" x 24")
Exterior Varnish
Acrylic Paint - Antique White and Georgia Clay
Stencil Creme Set - Heritage Colors
Africana Stencil
Two 3/8" Stencil Brushes
1" Flat Brush
Masking Tape

1. Paint the back of the piece of vinyl flooring. Let dry.

2. Position stencil along edge of the mat then secure with masking tape. Remove the film from the stencil creme with a paper towel. Dip the stencil brush into the Navy creme, then rub the brush on a paper towel to blend the paint in the bristles. Stencil the border design using a circular motion. Remember to use a different brush to stencil the Paprika colored parts of the pattern. Complete each section of the stencil pattern. Repeat pattern all the way around edge of the mat.

3. Stencil Navy triangles and Paprika swirls randomly in the center of the rug. Let dry for 3 days.

4. Thin Georgia Clay paint with water then brush over the entire surface of the cloth. Remove excess with a paper towel. You can add specks of color by spattering. Dip toothbrush bristles into the paint mix. Hold over the floor mat then run your finger across the bristles towards you. As the bristles pop back, specks of paint will fall over the surface. Let dry completely.

5. Brush surface with three coats of satin exterior varnish to seal. Let each coat of varnish dry before adding another.

Tape the stencil to edge of mat, then stencil one color at a time.

Stencil using a circular motion on open areas.

Run finger across bristles to spatter.

Delta Ceramcoat® Acrylic Paint, Stencil Magic® Creme, Stencils & Exterior Varnish

How to Play: For 2 Players

Place three "seeds" in each pit and decide who will start. The first player picks up all the pieces from one of his/her six pits then sows the pieces, one in each pit, around the board counter-clockwise including the *Kalaha* (end pit). If there are enough pieces, the player continues sowing into the pits on the opponent's side of the board. If a player's last piece lands in his own Kalaha, he gets another turn. A player may capture the pieces in the opponent's pit if his last piece is sown in an empty pit on his own side of the board. The player then gets to capture all the pieces in the opponent's pit and store them in his own Kalaha along with the capturing piece. When all six pits on one side of the board are empty, the game is over. The player who still has playing pieces in his own pits gets to put them in his own Kalaha. The winner is the player with the most "seeds" in his own Kalaha.

Mancala

by Kathleen George

Mancala is the common name given to a group of games from ancient Africa. Create your own version of this game with a styrofoam board and beautiful gem stone beads.

You will need:
18" x 6" x 1" Styrofoam
Fuzzi Felt - Red, Purple, Green, Blue, Orange and Yellow
Tacky Glue
36 Beads for "seeds"
Melon Baller
Pencil
Scissors

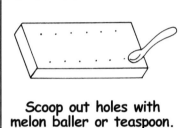

Scoop out holes with melon baller or teaspoon.

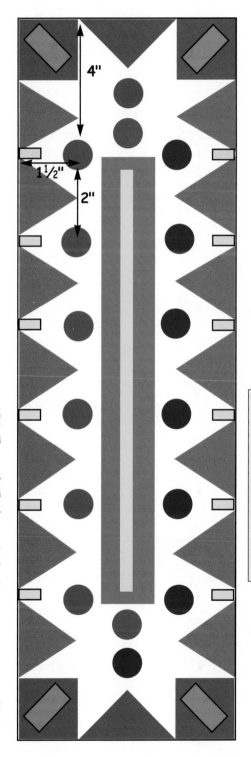

4"

1½"

2"

AFRICA

1. Make a pattern on a sheet of paper same size as styrofoam. Mark placement for holes 2" apart starting 4" from the top and 1½" from edge. Place the pattern on top of the styrofoam then push a sharp pencil through each dot into the styrofoam.

2. Remove the pattern, then scoop out shallow holes around the pencil point with either a melon baller or a teaspoon. Make an additional shallow hole at each end of the board. Smooth the edges with your fingertips.

3. Cut geometric shapes from fuzzi sheets then glue them to styrofoam board. Cut 2" strips of fuzzi sheet then cut into squares. Cut a square in half diagonally to make two triangles. You will need the following geometric shapes:

    1" Circles - 7 Blue, 2 Purple, 7 Green.
    2" Triangles - 14 Red, 2 Purple.
    Rectangles - 4 Orange 1" x ½"; 12 Yellow ¼" x ½";
                 1 Yellow 10" x 1", and 1 Purple 12" x 2".
    2" Squares - 4 Purple.

4. Glue the shapes to the top of the styrofoam and the circles in the pits. Cut 1" wide strips of Blue and glue around the edge.

5. Use beads to represent seeds as playing pieces.

Bemiss-Jason Fuzzi Sheets; Darice® Beads;
Dow Styrofoam® Brand Plastic Foam; Elmer's® Craft Bond ™ Tacky Glue

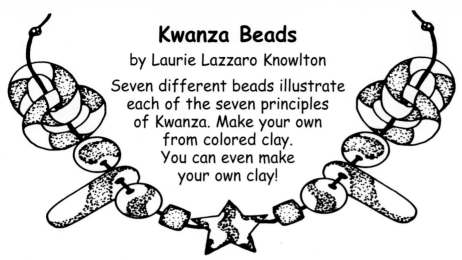

Kwanza Beads
by Laurie Lazzaro Knowlton

Seven different beads illustrate each of the seven principles of Kwanza. Make your own from colored clay. You can even make your own clay!

You will need		
Colored Glue	Cornstarch	Plastic Utensils
Flour	Mixing Bowl	Wax Paper

UJIMA = *Collective Work and Responsibility.*
These beads are made with a friend.

UMOJA = *Unity*
Roll snakes of several different colors. Twist the snakes together then slice. Colors are now unified.

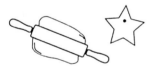

NIA = *Purpose.*
Roll a wad of dough flat then cut out a shape or use a mini cookie cutter to form bead.

KUJICHAGULIA = *Self Determination*
Make these beads in your own favorite color and shape.

UJAMMA = *Cooperative Economics*
Roll two different colors of snakes. Form the dough snakes into two interlocking circles.

IMANI =
Faith in oneself, the past, present & future.
Lay 3 sizes of flat circles on top of each other then press together to make a flat bead.

KUUMBA = *Creativity*
Roll two different colors together to form a swirl.

1. Pour one full bottle of colored glue into a plastic bag or small disposable bowl. Add one tablespoon of flour and one tablespoon of cornstarch.

2. Mix together by squeezing bag or stirring until the mixture forms a ball. If the mixture is too sticky add a little more flour or cornstarch.

3. Divide mixture into smaller balls then roll on wax paper to make a snake roll. Slice with a plastic knife. Twist two colors together if desired.

4. Pierce with a toothpick to make the hole for stringing. Let dry. Repeat using other colors.

Elmer's® Squeeze Creations™

Shekere

by Dawn Anderson for Arts & Crafts Kids Crafts Magazine

What's dancing without music? A Shekere is a musical African rattle made from a gourd. When the gourd dries out it is the seeds inside that rattle!

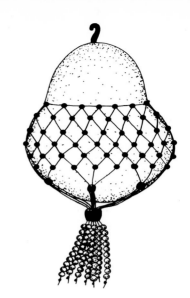

You will need:

Gourd, Paper Maché Gourd,
   or Styrofoam Ball & Dowel
45 yards of Cord or Yarn
125 Pony Beads

Large Eye Needle
Tape
Scissors
Ruler

1. For paper maché gourd only, cut three sides of a small square on bottom of gourd and insert a handful of beads. Tape or glue opening closed. Paint paper maché gold or orange.

2. Tie a length of cord loosely around the neck of the gourd where it begins to spread out. Tape ends onto the gourd out of the way. This is the collar cord. To determine length of tying cords, measure the gourd from the collar cord to the center of the gourd at the base. Add 5" for the tassel then multiply that number by six. For example, if the measurement is 8" you would add 5" for the tassel = 13" then multiply by 6 = 78". Cut 21 tying cords the same length.

3. Fold each tying cord in half and tie to collar cord in a lark's head knot. Space knots evenly around the collar cord.

    First Row: Take 1 cord from 1 set and the next cord from the next set then thread both through a bead. Push bead up until it is 1" from collar cord. Tie an overhand knot underneath to keep it in place. Repeat around the gourd.

    Second Row: Take 1 cord from 1 set beneath the bead and 1 cord from the next set. Thread both through a bead. Push bead up until it is about 1" from bead in row above. Tie an overhand knot underneath. Repeat second row all around the gourd until you reach the base of the gourd. Keeping the cords loose, thread three cords next to each other through a larger bead. Tie them together with an overhand knot beneath the bead. Repeat until you have seven groups.

4. Gather cords together at the center of the base of the gourd then tie with cord. Trim ends to same length as others. Cut a 12" piece of cord then wrap around cords first in one direction then in the other. Thread end through a large eye needle and pull through center of wrapped cords to secure.

5. Thread 10 beads onto each length of cord, then tie a knot under the last one. Thread 10 beads onto each end of collar cord. Tie a knot beneath last one.

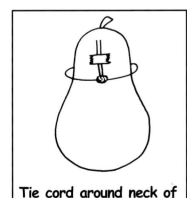

Tie cord around neck of gourd. Tape the ends.

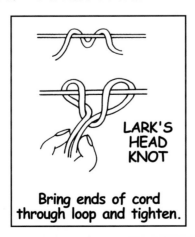

LARK'S HEAD KNOT

Bring ends of cord through loop and tighten.

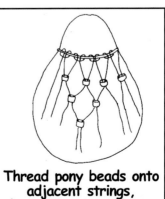

Thread pony beads onto adjacent strings, alternating on each row.

Wrap tassel with cord.

Darice® Cord, Pony Beads & Large Eye Needle

Dance Mask

by Patty Cox

Traditional ceremonial African dance masks were worn to influence hunting, intellectual and spiritual needs, and even for comedy. They were made out of wood then decorated with berries, shells, mirrors, horn and copper.

You will need:

White Glue	Feathers
Yellow Confetti	4 Red Wood Beads
Acrylic Paint - Georgia Clay, Ivory and Black	1" Flat Paintbrush
Crackle Medium	Masking Tape
5" Styrofoam Disk	12" Black Crêpe Paper Streamer
Balloon	Cardboard

1. Blow up the balloon to the approximate size of a head and tie off. Place balloon on a bowl to steady.

2. Tear or cut the newspaper into 1½" x 6" strips.

3. Mix 2 parts glue to 1 part water in a disposable container. Dip newspaper strips into the mixture then slide strips through fingers to remove excess. Cover the front half of the balloon with two layers of the strips of newspaper.

4. Cut a 2" triangle nose from the cardboard, fold in center then glue in place with moistened newspaper strips. Add two or three more layers of strips over the face. Let dry.

5. Pop the balloon and pull away from the mask. Trim uneven edges from the mask.

6. Paint mask black. Let dry, then paint with a generous coat of crackle medium. Let dry for about 20 minutes.

7. Paint Ivory over the crackle medium. Watch the cracks form as the paint dries!

8. Paint designs as shown with Georgia Clay and Black, or create your own designs.

9. Cut styrofoam disk in half then glue one half to the inside of the mask at the top. Glue feathers into the top edge of the styrofoam then confetti over the base of the feathers. Glue a black crêpe paper streamer over base of confetti at the top of the mask. Tuck ends in at the back of the mask. Glue four red beads on top of the crêpe paper band.

Cover balloon with strips of newspaper.

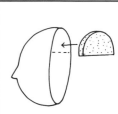

Glue half of styrofoam disk into the back of the mask.

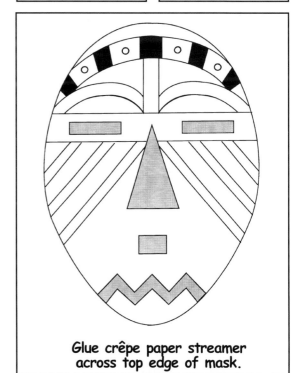

Glue crêpe paper streamer across top edge of mask.

Bemiss-Jason & Spectra® Art Crêpe™; Darice® Feathers & Wood Beads; Delta Ceramcoat® Acrylic Paint & Crackle Medium; Dow Styrofoam® Brand Plastic Foam; Elmer's® School Glue

Join Our Craft Adventure to
JAPAN

Discover Oriental crafting traditions when you make:

- Origami Kimono and Pinwheel
- Temari Balls • Origami Fish
- Watercolor Windsock
- Plum Blossom Fan

Temari Ball

by Kathleen George

Temari Balls are one of the most intricate and beautiful Japanese designs. Designs are made by weaving multi-colored threads into exquisite patterns.

You will need:
3" Styrofoam Ball
30 - 40 yards of Black Yarn
Assorted Bright Colored Yarn
Two 1" Round Head Plastic Pins
9½" x ½" Strip of Paper
Large Eye Plastic Needle
Scissors

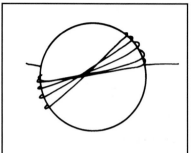

Wrap yarn around the styrofoam ball.

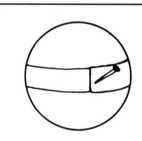

Use a strip of paper and pins to mark the center front and back.

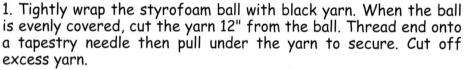

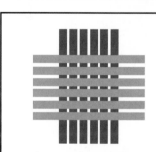

Make a second band of color around the ball across the first band.

1. Tightly wrap the styrofoam ball with black yarn. When the ball is evenly covered, cut the yarn 12" from the ball. Thread end onto a tapestry needle then pull under the yarn to secure. Cut off excess yarn.

2. Fold the 9½" strip of paper in half. Place around the center of the ball. Place a pin in the ball where the ends of the paper meet and at the fold. Remove the paper.

3. Thread 2 yards of colored yarn onto the needle. Pull under the black yarn, bringing it up at a pin. Wrap the yarn around the center of the ball being careful not to pull the end of the yarn out. Continue wrapping until you have a band of solid color around the center. Secure the end of the yarn under the black yarn at the point where you started. Carefully cut off excess.

4. Wrap 2-3 rows of a second color on either side of the first band Continue until the band of colors is as wide as you like.

5. Make a band of color around the ball in the other direction. You can make the areas where the bands cross more interesting by weaving the yarn through the first band instead of just wrapping it over the top.

6. To make a tassel, wrap yarn 10-20 times around cardboard about 4" wide. Slip a 6" piece of yarn under the loops then tie tightly. This is the top of the tassel. Cut the loops opposite the top then wrap a contrasting color of yarn around the tassel near the top. Tie to secure then trim uneven ends.

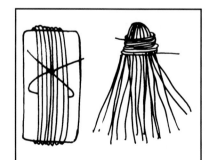

Wrap yarn around card to make a tassel.

Bemiss-Jason Assorted Yarns Dispenser & Needle;
Dow Styrofoam® Brand Plastic Foam

Watercolor Windsock

by Cecille Diez

Water color painting is an important Japanese art technique. It is often used to create the delicate brush strokes which form the letters and symbols of Japanese script.

You will need:	Glue
Rice Paper*, or	Brushes
Lightweight Paper	Round Ring or Hoop
Water-Color Brush Pens	String
Water-Color Paints	*36" x 48" needed for a
Spray Bottle of Water	12" Embroidery Hoop

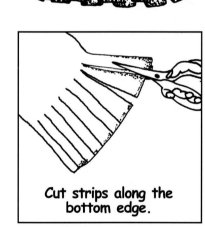

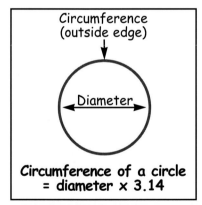

Circumference (outside edge)

Diameter

Circumference of a circle = diameter x 3.14

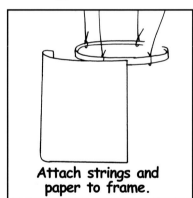

Attach strings and paper to frame.

Cut strips along the bottom edge.

1. Measure around the outside of your frame to determine how wide your paper should be. Add approximately ½" to overlap where the edges will meet then decide how long you would like your windsock to be. Cut your paper to these measurements.
2. Using the fish design for inspiration, draw a light sketch of your design onto the paper. Color in the desired areas with watercolor brush pens, or watercolor paint. When finished, spray entire design lightly with water. Watch how water colors bleed and blend to create a completely new effect of pattern and color!
3. Cut a fringe along the bottom edge of the paper to catch the breeze.
4. Tie three lengths of string or ribbon to the frame spacing them so they are about the same distance apart. Knot the opposite ends together. Fold the top of the paper down 1", wrap it around the frame then either glue or tape in place.
5. Hang near a window indoors to catch the breeze and enjoy!

Elmer's® Craft Bond™ Paper Glue; Prang® Washable Markers™ & Watercolors

Origami Kimono and Pinwheel

Courtesy of FamilyFun Magazine

Toys are easy to make by simply folding paper! This is a traditional Japanese art called origami. It is also used to teach accuracy patience, and concentration.

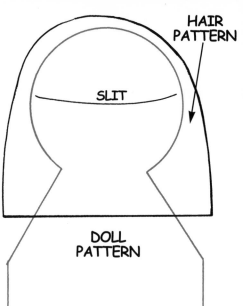

HAIR PATTERN

SLIT

DOLL PATTERN

Kimono

1. Cut doll's body from posterboard. Cut wig and 6" x 3/8" rectangle from black paper.
2. Draw a face on the doll's head with markers. To make Kimono, fold down one edge of the 6" paper square 3/8" for collar. Color the collar.
3. Cut slit in the wig and place on doll's head. Place the doll on the center of the kimono with the collar face down at the top. Fold the top corner of the kimono down over shoulder toward the front of the doll, then fold the piece on the side over the dolls body. Repeat on the other side. Wrap a 3/4" x 6" sash around the doll and tape ends together at the back.

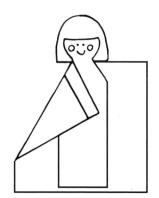

Fold paper down over the shoulder and across from side.

You will need:
Origami Paper
Glue Stick
Pushpin
Thin Dowel
Posterboard
Construction Paper
Black Paper
Scissors
Markers

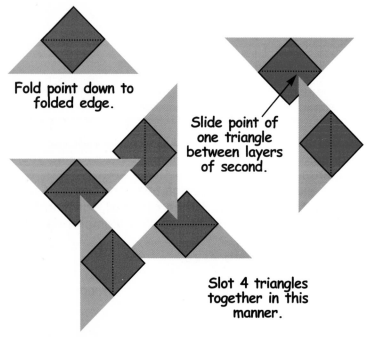

Fold point down to folded edge.

Slide point of one triangle between layers of second.

Slot 4 triangles together in this manner.

Pinwheel

1. Fold one sheet of paper in half diagonally. Crease lightly along the fold. Fold in half again, make a light crease then unfold.
2. Fold one layer of top point down to fold and secure with glue. Repeat steps 1 and 2 with three more pieces of paper.
3. Aligning the folded edge of one unit with the creased center of another, slip one unit into another as shown. Secure with a spot of glue. Tuck the point of the third unit into the second in the same way. Slide the point of the fourth unit into the third, while at the same time sliding the point of the first unit into the fourth. Secure with glue.
4. To complete use a pushpin to attach the pinwheel to either a dowel or to the eraser end of a pencil.

Bemiss-Jason Spectra Construction & Origami Paper;
Elmer's® Craft Bond Glue Stick; Fiskars® Student Scissors.

Origami Fish
by Brenda Spitzer

Create a mosaic fish picture from small pieces of folded paper. The fish is an important symbol in Japan because fishing is very important to the Japanese economy.

You will need:
Metallic Paper - Green, Blue and Magenta
Blue Two-Tone Paper
Decorative Glue
Decorative Scissors
36" Mini Corrugated Blue Border
Ruler
Pencil
12" x 18" Turquoise Posterboard

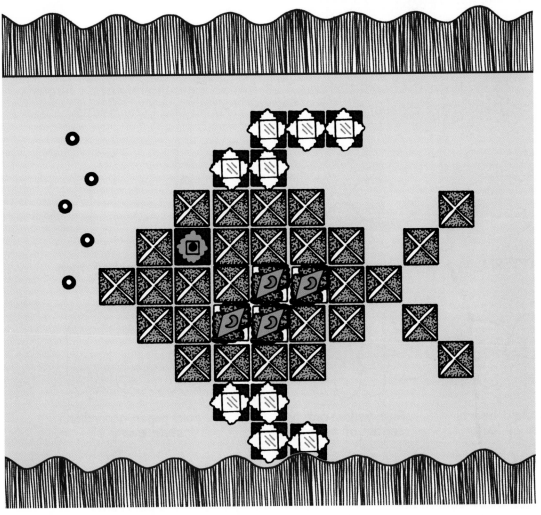

GREEN

Fold the corners toward the center.

MAGENTA

Fold points back at an angle to form diamond shape.

BLUE

Fold points toward the center then fold back to edge.

JAPAN

1. Using decorative, or plain scissors, cut the metallic paper into the number of required 2" x 2" squares as follows: Green - 27; Blue - 9; Magenta - 4; Lt. Blue/Dk. Blue duet - 1.

2. With the White side facing up, fold the corners of the Green and Blue squares toward center. For the Blue squares only, fold the points back out again. With the Magenta side facing up, fold the points of the squares toward the center, then back at an angle to form a diamond shape.

3. Lightly draw diagonal lines from corner to corner across the Turquoise posterboard to find the center. Mark with a pencil then starting at the center. Glue squares in place following the chart.

4. Glue fluted border to the top and bottom edges of the posterboard.

5. Draw fish bubbles and decorate fish with glitter and ice-a-delic glue. Let dry.

Bemiss-Jason Fadeless™ Duet & Metallic Paper & Mini-Flute Bordette; Elmer's® Fun Dimensions™ Ice-A-Delic & Glitter Gel; Fiskars® Paper Edgers & Ruler

Plum Blossom Fan

by Patty Cox

Cherry blossoms have been cherished for centuries by the Japanese as a symbol of their national character. Decorate a folded paper fan with these highly prized, beautiful blossoms.

You will need:

12" x 18" Fadeless Metallic Paper - Fuchsia	Hole and Heart Punches
Green Crêpe Paper	Paper Crimper
Construction Paper - Pink and Yellow	Glue
3 Iridescent Chenille Stems	Glitter Glue
Decorative Scissors	Corrugated Cardboard
	Straight Pins
	Misc. Embellishments - Sequins, Raffia and Pony Beads

LEAF PATTERN

Twist leaf in center.

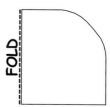

Fold paper in half then cut an arch at top.

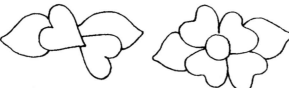

Glue 4 punched hearts to center of leaf.

Glue yellow dot to center of hearts.

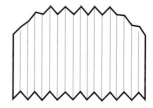

Fold paper accordion style every 1".

1. Fold 18" paper in half. Cut an arc on top and sides with edger scissors as shown in diagram.
2. Make accordion folds in fan paper every 1". Run folded paper through crimper at an angle. Bend and lightly crease lower 2" of folded paper. This area will be the handle. Open folds.
3. Punch a round hole in each 1" section, about ½" from top edge.
4. Make 12 Blossoms: Cut leaves from crêpe paper. Twist the center. Punch four pink hearts then glue to center of leaf as shown. Punch then glue a yellow dot in the center. Glue blossoms on fan, above handle crease. Make dots around flowers with glitter glue then glue sequins between the dots. Allow glue to dry.
5. Refold fan then wrap chenille stems around the handle. Fold an 18" strand of straw raffia in half then wrap it around the handle. Tie pony beads and sequins on the strands.
6. Temporarily place fan on corrugated cardboard. Apply glue to each outward fold on fan back. Lay fan on a sheet of pink construction paper. Stick straight pins in each inward fold to hold fan in position until glue dries. Remove the fan from cardboard then trim the backing paper with the decorative scissors approximately ¾" from the edge of the fan.

Bemiss-Jason Metallic Fadeless™ Paper, Crêpe Paper & Spectra Construction Paper; Darice® Chenille Stems & Embellishments; Elmer's® Fun Dimensions™ Glitter Glue; Fiskars® Paper Edgers, Paper Crimper & Punches

Travel Briefcase
Courtesy of FamilyFun Magazine

Store your momentoes in this folder-style, 3-D travel briefcase. Just one of these will hold ticket stubs, stickers, postcards and other souvenirs you may have picked up on your travels.

You will need:
2 Colored Cardboard
  Report Covers
Glue
Stick-on Velcro Fasteners
Large Manila Envelopes

1. Cut a pair of "U" shaped handles and two 1½" x 18" straps from one cardboard report cover.

2. Glue handles to the inside of the front and back cover of the second report cover. Wrap the straps around the outside of the cover, aligning with the top edge, then glue in place. Fold ends over the top so that they overlap the front. Attach the stick-on velcro fasteners to the ends of the straps.

3. Glue a large open envelope to the inside cover to store photographs, then fill the suitcase with manila folders for storing ticket stubs, brochures and other souvenirs.

PATTERN FOR
HANDLES
CUT 2

Elmer's® Craft Bond™ Tacky Glue

Around the World Game

by Kim Thomas

It doesn't take 80 days to go around the world any more. In fact, it's amazing how far you can go without even leaving your home. Test your knowledge about the flags of the different countries you've visited and more! You'll find this game a fun way to jog your memory.

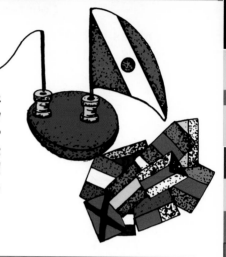

You will need:

Four Split Pigeon Eggs
Eight ½" Wood Spools
Four 1" Wood Button Plugs
Eight Craft Matchsticks
Magnet Strips
24 White Index Cards
Heavyweight Paper, or
  24 Colored Index Cards
24" of Waxed Linen
28 Corks - #2
28 Thumb Tacks

56 Wiggle Eyes - 5mm
Acrylic Paint - White, Black,
  Yellow, Green, Red, Orange,
  Dark Blue, Ocean Reef Blue
Sailboat Punch
Decorative Scissors
Fine Tip Markers
Colored Pencils
Water Based Varnish
Tacky Glue
Small Sponge
Paintbrush

Rules of the Game

2-4 Players sit at a table or on the floor in a circle with the fish grouped in the center to form a fish pond. Deal the cards, face down to each player. The first player chooses the top card and says country name aloud. He then pushes his boat into the fish pond and with his magnetic fishing pole, catches all the colors of fish he feels are in the flag. He looks at the card. If he has caught all the correct colors in the flag, he shows the other players, returns the fish to the pond and keeps the flag face up. If he is incorrect he calls "Set sail for (the name of the country)". All remaining players go fishing at this point until someone has the correct colors, at which time he calls out "Land Ahoy"! (name of the country). the player with the correct colors gets to keep the flag.

If no one can come up with the correct colors, the flag is shown to everyone then put back on the bottom of the player's stack. Play continues in a clockwise direction until all cards are face up. The player with the most flags wins!

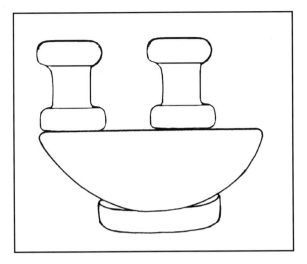

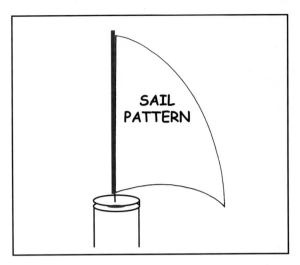

Sailboats - Make 4: Glue one spool to the center of the flat side of the egg and one spool to the narrow end. Paint one boat of each color White, Red, Yellow and Blue.

Base - Make 4: Paint button plugs Ocean Reef Blue then sponge with White. Glue one to base of each egg.

Sails - Make 4: Cut 4 sails from medium weight cardboard. Draw a design on the sail with markers then glue to one end of a matchstick. Glue matchsticks into spools.

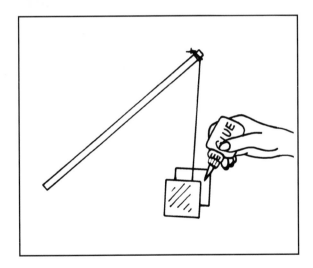

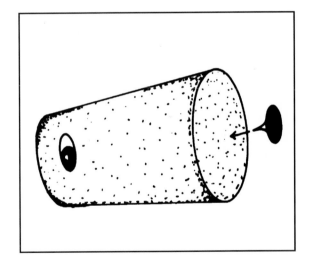

Fishing Poles - Tie 6" of waxed linen to one end of matchstick. Trim to 4". Cut two ¼" squares from magnet strip then glue together over the end of waxed linen.

Fish - Paint 4 corks in each of the following colors: White, Black, Yellow, Green, Red, Blue and Orange. Let dry. Push one tack into narrow end of each cork. Glue eyes in place.

Flag Cards - Copy 24 flag patterns found throughout this book onto White index cards. Color with crayons or markers. Glue to colored index cards, or heavyweight paper. Write the name of the country on White paper, cut out with decorative scissors then glue to the back of the card. Laminate the cards if desired.

Darice® Wood Craft; Delta Ceramcoat® acrylic Paint & Varnish; Elmer's® Craft Bond™ Tacky Glue; Fiskars® Paper Edgers & Punch

HOME AGAIN

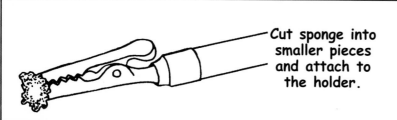

Travel Memories
by Tracia Ledford-Williams

Make an album of photo pages of your vacation photos. Don't forget to write captions on your pages, then you'll always be able to look back and remember exactly where you were and what you did!

You will need:
Album Cover
Vacation Stencil
Paper Paint - Raspberry Patch, Chocolate Kiss, Garden Green, White, Orange Sizzle, Beach Ball Blue, Sunburst Yellow
Stencil Sponge & Holder
Decorative Scissors
Acid Free Glue
Hole Punch
Tape, or Sticky Dots
Black Fine Permanent Marker
Acid Free Album Page

Cut sponge into smaller pieces and attach to the holder.

1. Place the stencil on the album cover and secure with dots or tape. Cut sponge into 4 or 5 small pieces, clip to the stencil holder then sponge Blue paper paint around the edges to create the wave design. Dip sponge into White then sponge on clouds.

2. Dip a clean sponge into Yellow paint then White. Lightly sponge on color for sand.

3. Add additional stencil designs using following colors:

    Tree Trunk, Boat and Umbrella Pole - Brown.
    Palm Tree Fronds - Green.
    Sail - Yellow and Orange.
    Umbrella - Orange and Sun - Yellow.
Add tiny Raspberry dots to sail and top of umbrella.

4. Decorate an album page in the same manner. To add photos, position the stencil rectangle over the part of the photograph you wish to use. Trace around the area with a pencil then cut photo with decorative scissors. Glue photo in place inside the stenciled frame.

5. Punch an assortment of paper shapes from colored paper and use to decorate pages if desired.

Attach stencil to page with stencil dots or tape.

Delta Cherished Memories™ Stencils, Acid-Free Paper Paint™, Stencil Buddy™ & Stencil Sponges; Dixon Redisharp® Permanent Markers; Fiskars® Paper Edgers & Punches

Luggage Pocket Page
by Patty Cox

Finding a place to store souvenirs won't be a problem with this luggage pocket page. It's a perfect fit for a 3-ring binder album.

You will need:

Construction Paper -
  Red, Yellow, Green,
  Blue and Brown
Decorative Scissors
Punches
Glue
Re-Positionable Glue
  Stick

Permanent Markers
Chalk - Brown
Alphabet Beads
Misc. Sequins, Wiggle
  Eyes

Optional: Decoupage Sealer

1. Fold suitcase-colored construction paper in half. Cut out keeping folded edge at the bottom. Cut two straps from the same color of paper.

2. Draw stitch lines on straps with the marker. Color the handle. To make a well traveled look of leather, rub chalk along the edges of the straps and handle.

3. Use geometric shapes as patterns for cutting out photos to decorate your pocket page. Use straight or decorative edge scissors.

4. Open suitcase. Apply repositionable glue around the outer edge of the case. Allow glue to set for 60 seconds before closing the case.

5. Stack three, colored pieces of construction paper together. Make a mark 3" down on the right hand side then draw a line from this point to the upper left hand corner. Cut along the line through all three thicknesses. Layer cut sheets on a full sheet as shown. **Note,** the center piece will be turned in the opposite direction. Trim bottom of sheets to the same length as the backing sheet.

6. Glue each angled sheet along the bottom and side to make the pocket. Punch 3 holes (spaced to fit an album) on left side of the pocket page.

7. Decorate the pockets and suitcase with paper punches, stickers, sequins, alphabet beads, rubber stamps, wiggle eyes and markers. Shade the edges of the pocket pages with chalk.

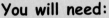

SUITCASE PATTERN

PLACE ON FOLD

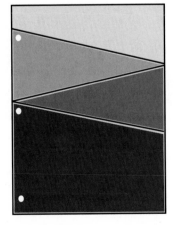

Layer the three angled sheets on top of the full sheet. Trim to fit at the bottom. Glue angled sheets in place along the bottom and sides.

Thread alphabet beads together. Attach to strap.

HOME AGAIN

Bemiss-Jason Spectra® Construction Paper; Elmer's® Craft Bond™ Tacky Glue & Re-Positionable Glue Stick; Fiskars® Paper Edgers, Student Scissors & Punches

Pencil Pals

by Kim Thomas

Top your pencils with these figures as a reminder of the wonderful people you met during your travels around the world.

You will need:
*Wood Pencil Pot
*Pencil
*20mm Natural
  Wood Bead
*Two 10mm Natural
  Wood Beads
Red Crayon
Fine Tip Black
  Permanent Marker
Acrylic Paint
Tacky Glue
Paintbrush
Scissors
Needle & Thread
*For each pencil topper

1. Paint beads appropriate color for skin tones and the pencil pots with colors to complement the clothing you choose. Glue the 20 mm bead to the bottom of the upside-down pot. Apply cheek color with a small stencil brush and stencil paint, or color with a red crayon. Add two black dots for eyes. The small beads are glued to each side of the pot for arms.
2. Glue ribbon or fabric to pot for clothing. To make dresses, run a gathering stitch ⅛" from the top edge of the fabric. Pull tightly around doll's neck, tie off then glue together at back.
3. Glue hair to the head then trim as needed. Paint wood turnings to be used for hats, or glue pre-made hats or flowers on top of head. The additional supplies for each pencil pal are listed below.

CHINA
Black Wool (Hair)
Floral Ribbon
3 Babies Breath
Florets
5mm Red Pom Pom

AFRICA
¾" Wood Bowl (Hat)
1" x 12" Teal Mosaic
Fabric (Dress)
Black Curly Hair
Multi-Colored Seed
Beads for Necklace

MEXICO
¾" X 3½" of
Striped Fabric
Black Wool (Hair)
1½" Straw
Sombrero

UK
¾" Wood Wheel (Hat)
Plaid Fabric
Dark Blond Curly
Wool Hair
4" x ⅜" Plaid Ribbon
Two 7mm Yellow
Pom Poms

Darice® Woodcraft Beads & Pencil Pots™; Delta Ceramcoat® Acrylic Paint;
Elmer's® Craft Bond™ Tacky Glue; Fiskars® Scissors